MIND MANUAL

Train Your Mind, Transform Your Vibe

By April Norris CHt

with Dustyn Brown

Illustrated by Lydia Kurshuk

MIND MANUAL

Editor: Elizabeth Bergman
Illustrations: Lydia Kurshuk
Graphic Design Director: Joanna Blandon
Production Coordinator: Marlene Lopez

Paperback ISBN: 979-8-9938551-3-4
Hardcover ISBN: 979-8-9938551-2-7

Printed in United States of America

www.mindmoodvibe.com/mmvpress/mindmanual

Dedication

This book is dedicated to...

The visionaries.
Who have a dream that they yearn to bring to life.

The healers.
Who remind us of our wholeness.

The artists.
Who share beauty as if life depends on it.

The leaders.
Who generously *teach others to fish*.

The magical.
Who have minds full of wonder and curiosity.

Acknowledgements

To my team...

My heart is full when I think of how you helped me bring this dream forth.
May you feel pride & joy over our creation.

Dustyn, your humor and exquisite idea architecture brought a rough and unruly manuscript to life.

Lydia, your profound imagination and artistry imbued a playfulness and sparkle to each page.

Marlene, Susan and AJ, your wisdom and brilliance brought clarity and ease to the challenges along the way.

Elizabeth, you made the most challenging part of the book-writing process a breeze.
Your attention to detail and rigor with citations tethered this book to truth.

Dr. Merlino, Dr. Del Valle, and Dr. Gaines, your partnership has been a blessing. Your work is a vital bridge to the future of mind-body medicine, transforming both care and education.

Lauren and Brad, from students to colleagues to friends. It has been a pleasure to watch you blossom into gifted healers.

My mom Roberta, dad William, sisters Lancy and Meredith, and niece Jacqueline.
You gave me everything I needed to become myself.

Joanna, my partner and love. You sweetened the journey with unwavering support every step of the way.

I love you all.

Table of Contents

Introduction:
Train Your Mind, Transform Your Vibe

What if the secret to a life of joy, connection, and fulfillment wasn't found in external circumstances or achievements, but in the invisible frequency of our thoughts?

Everything in the universe, including our thoughts and emotions, vibrates in its own unique way. Much like adjusting a radio dial, we can shift our mental tuning to transform how we experience life.

Many people don't realize how profoundly their mindset impacts their day-to-day lives. Our thoughts shape our reality, setting the tone for everything we encounter. When we elevate our mindset and live in alignment with our values, we naturally invite expansive, life-affirming experiences and increase the likelihood of realizing our dreams. We feel free to follow our bliss.

On the other hand, misalignment and negative thought patterns keep us trapped in cycles of doubt, fear, and frustration. It can feel as if life is just a series of struggles and bad luck.

The good news? The mind is the ultimate tool for shaping your life. It converts external stimuli into your personal, high-definition version of reality.

The mind is endlessly adaptable, allowing you to consciously shift your perspective and reshape your world. When we learn to use it effectively, we open ourselves to new realities filled with joy, gratitude, and purpose.

A Personal Beginning

As children, we naturally vibrate at higher frequencies—filled with imagination, curiosity, and joy. But over time, and sometimes all at once, external influences cause us to hide our authentic selves. Mastering the mind involves shedding limiting beliefs, rewriting our internal narrative, and returning to our authentic vibe.

I grew up with young parents who hadn't fully processed their own emotional pain before becoming parents themselves. Residual trauma and cultural conditioning shaped their worldview, and mine. My father's childhood was marked by poverty, instability, grief and a relentless search for security. My mother grew up surrounded by unspoken trauma and invisible wounds which led her into anger and emotional chaos.

They did their best, and I deeply honor their courage. For many years, my dad worked two full-time jobs as a janitor to support us. Even without much sleep, he remained the hardest working, most positive person around. He's my hero. My mom is my greatest teacher and catalyzed my passion for mind and mood fitness. I love them deeply.

All that said, growing up in an environment of shame, scarcity and rage taught me that emotions were dangerous, self-care was selfish, and survival was the primary goal. As my parents searched for security and answers, the Southern Baptist Church literally came knocking on our door and introduced our family into a world of dogma, fear, hellfire and judgment. Those stories are for another book though.

The Inner Imprint of Trauma

So many of our core beliefs are shaped before we even know we're forming them.

I share the details of my family's struggles not to dwell in pain, but to show how deeply our early environments influence the way we view ourselves and the world. The emotional chaos and survival mentality I grew up with left a lasting imprint on my nervous system and my sense of worth.

"Trauma is not what happened to us, but what happened inside us as a result"[1] —Dr. Gabor Maté.

Trauma isn't just about dramatic events, it's about the meaning we attach, the emotional residue we carry, and the unconscious programming that follows us into adulthood.

The vast majority of people experience some form of trauma at some time in their lives. Most of us are carrying stories we didn't consciously choose— stories about not being safe, not being enough, not being allowed to feel. These stories become default settings in the subconscious mind. And until we become aware of them, they run the show.

From Breakdown to Breakthrough

My transformation didn't begin in a moment of glory. It began with failure, grief, betrayal, and loss. I lost my health, my home, close relationships and my financial stability. I faced a misdiagnosed autoimmune illness, went bankrupt, and felt the weight of a reality that was my worst nightmare.

And yet, in that dark space, I made a choice. I created my first vision board. I began observing and guiding my own thoughts. I discovered how my internal world was shaping everything.

It wasn't a straight line. Healing required confronting my own shadow, releasing judgment, and choosing new patterns. But that inner work led to awe-inspiring experiences:

swimming with wild dolphins around the world, holding the Dalai Lama's hand, soulful conversations about manifestation on a yacht with John Travolta to name a few. I built my dream tiny home. I met my amazing life partner. I helped others heal—and healed myself in the process.

The inner work wasn't a quick or easy process, but it opened the doors to wondrous events. Upon looking back, I realize that these surreal experiences came right off the pages of my vision board.

The correlation between doing difficult inner work and later receiving the gifts of that healing became very clear to me. I've learned first-hand that healing and manifesting are closely correlated. An open mind and heart allow you to notice the opportunities the world presents to you and give you the intuition and courage to receive them.

All of this points to one simple truth which is the essence of this book: *no matter the circumstances, the mind is magical and can transform itself.*

Why I Wrote This Book

I share my story not for sympathy, but for resonance. If you've struggled, doubted, or longed for something more, this book is for you.

This is a guide for retraining your mind and reclaiming your vibe. It is a synthesis of research, experience, and deep soul work. It blends science with soul, psychology with frequency, practical tools with poetic truth.

You'll learn how to work with your subconscious, release inherited thought patterns, and tune into the vibration of possibility. You'll discover how to design a reality that reflects your highest values and deepest desires.

How to Use This Book

Let it be personal. Mark it up. Highlight what resonates. Skip ahead and come back again. Use colored pencils to color the pictures—or draw your own. Treat it like a conversation with your higher self. This is not a rigid doctrine. It's a permission slip. A playground. A portal.

Remember: theory is valuable, but transformation comes from practice, reflection, and compassion. Be kind to yourself. Let love be your lens. And know that every small mental shift has the potential to unlock a new reality.

Final Note

The mind is magical. It can be re-trained, re-wired, and re-tuned. Healing and manifesting are not

separate; they are reflections of the same vibration. By reading this book, you are choosing to become conscious. That choice alone shifts everything.
So take what resonates. Leave the rest. Stay curious. Stay open. And most of all, enjoy the ecstatic ahas waiting for you along the way.

A Living Book for a Living Mind

This book synthesizes what has come before; many different perspectives, ideas, and approaches. It is alive with questions, insights, and possibilities.

I am determined not to take myself so seriously as to presume (1) this is the whole story, or (2) that mistakes have not been made. Your feedback is welcome. Once published, I'll take great care to provide updates, corrections, and evolving insights that emerge from continued exploration into the nature of consciousness and the mind.

Humans continually adapt and evolve, and so does our understanding.

Whether or not our paths ever cross in person, I'm grateful for this connection we now share, and all that you've set into motion by reading this book.

I wish you peace, love, prosperity, good vibes, and a life filled with the magic that comes from mastery of the mind.

> *"The mind isn't a cage, it's a stage. Train the actors, and the play transforms."*
>
> **April Norris**

Threshholds of Perception:
A Ritual of Awakening

Take a slow, full breath. This isn't just a foreword. It's a frequency shift. A subtle, sacred initiation. As your eyes move across these words, let your mind soften, your curiosity widen, and your awareness deepen. You are stepping across a threshold, out of ordinary perception and into a new dimension of understanding.

We are living in a time of breathtaking revelations. An age where the fabric of reality itself seems to be peeling back, offering glimpses of deeper truths once confined to myth and speculation. Are we living in a simulation? Very possibly.

Quantum physicists now whisper of parallel worlds brushing against our own, as though reality has become a hall of infinite reflections. Holographic theory and quantum computing, with shimmering promise, hint that reality is not a solid stage but a web of probabilities. One where the observer shapes the scene.

Orbs drift in the sky, teasing the edges of perception, daring us to question the limits of what we call *real*. Meanwhile, artificial intelligence simulates language, creativity, even curiosity—yet Sir Roger Penrose reminds us: computation is not consciousness. Algorithms predict but do not dream. They process but do not ponder.[2] We stand at a threshold, blinking, as if we've wandered into Plato's Cave, the shadows on the wall growing sharper while the source of light remains just beyond reach. And yet, with all these wonders swirling around us, we risk losing the most extraordinary frontier of all; the mind itself.

Because amidst the noise of technological breakthroughs and cosmic riddles, clarity of thought is more vital than ever. A steady mind. A good mood. A high vibration. Not just poetic ideals, but essential tools for navigating a reality that seems to be rewriting itself in real time.

This book is not just a guide; it's a call to reclaim your mental power in an age of distraction and awe. To sharpen your perception. To cultivate resilience. To explore the vastness within you, just as profoundly as those peering into the vastness beyond.

So, let this be your moment of conscious entry. You are not just reading. You are attuning. Aligning. Choosing.

The future isn't just arriving—it's being shaped by minds like yours.

TEZCATLIPOCA:
MIRROR OF THE HIDDEN MIND

What is Mind?

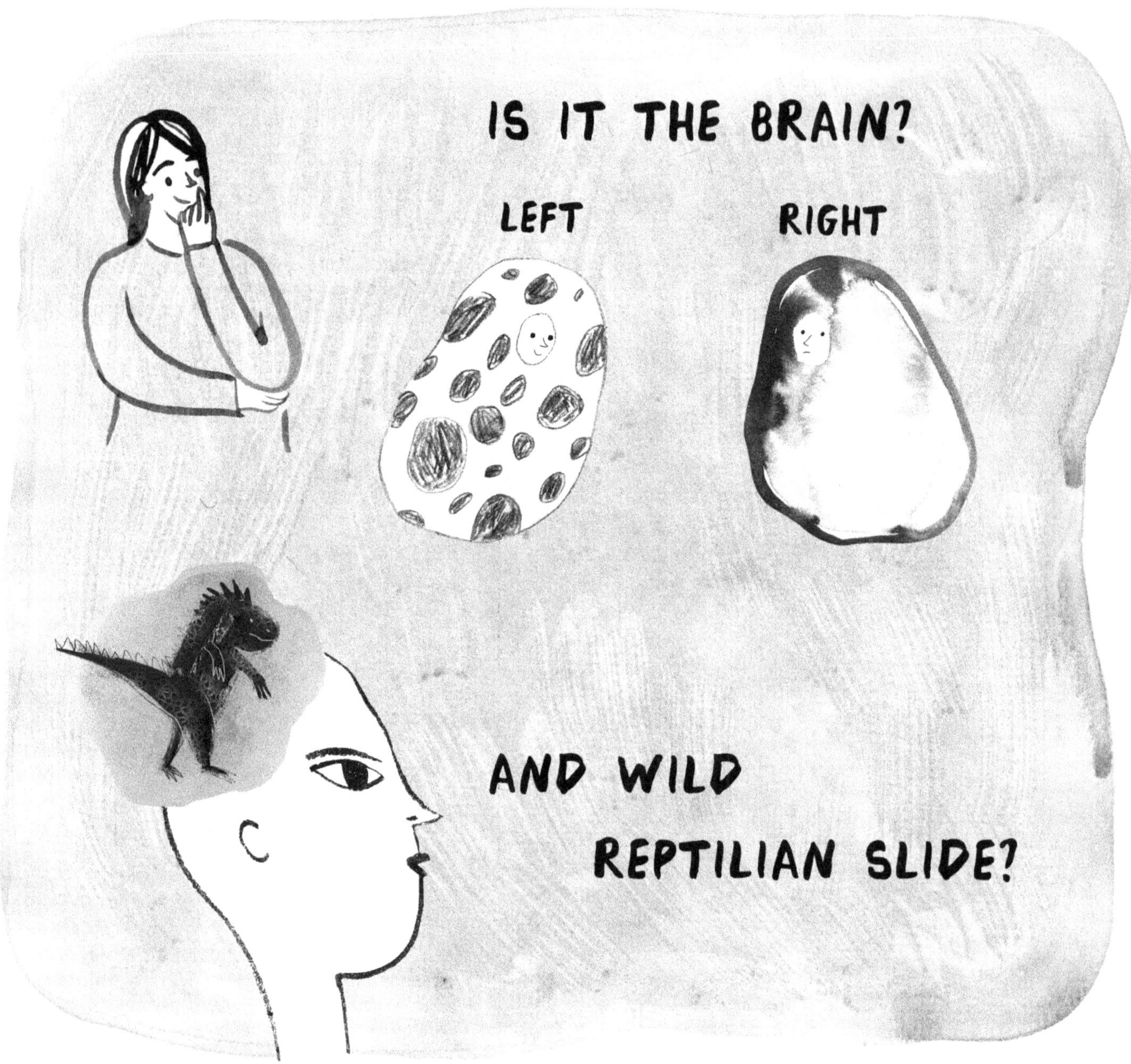

IS MIND FOUND IN NATURE?

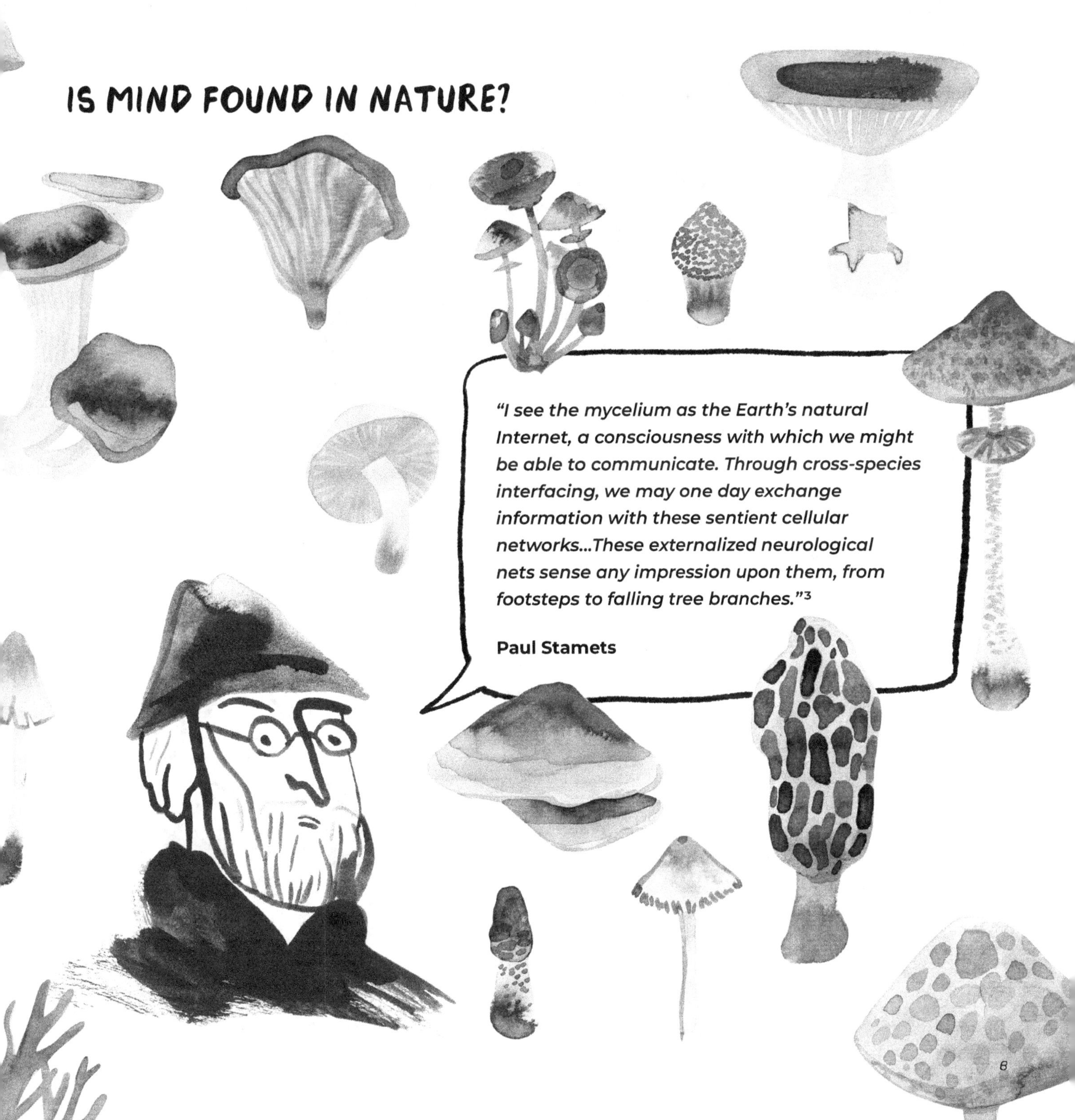

CAN ROBOTS HAVE A MIND?

IS MIND BEYOND TIME AND SPACE?

The mind represents a mysterious world of thinking and feeling that goes beyond the biology of the physical brain and links us with the greater universe.

Let's go on a journey together to uncover and understand the mind—*and* learn how you can harness its potential to make meaningful changes in your life.

To understand any concept, we can start with a dictionary. For *mind* the Oxford English Dictionary lists over 100 definitions. The myriad meanings of mind range from intentions and opinions to the Universe or almighty God. That's more range than Mariah Carey.

Daniel Siegel, a clinical professor of psychiatry at UCLA, defines the mind as "an embodied and relational process that regulates the flow of energy and information."[5] This definition emphasizes the mind's connection to both the body and relationships, highlighting its dynamic role in managing how energy and information move within and between individuals.

Let's define mind as:

The intelligence that allows us to perceive, think, learn, feel, focus, imagine, dream, intuit, decide, remember and connect.

MIND: A WORD THAT OPENS DOORS

Pay no mind, and you miss the moment.

Speak your mind, and you reclaim your voice.

Be in a good state of mind, and life blooms from the inside out.

Be in your right mind, and you stand in clarity and truth.

Change your mind, and you change your future.

Make up your mind, and step right into alignment.

Say "I mind!" and you honor your boundaries and worth.

The word mind is more than a noun. It's a verb, a guide, a gateway. It can signal awareness, memory, presence, choice, concern and resolve. It is where the story lives and where the rewrite starts.

Our evolving understanding of the mind has an interesting history. Let's explore…

The origin and evolution of mind remain unknown, shrouded in mystery and myth, suggesting the existence of advanced prehistoric civilizations with technologies we have yet to comprehend.

PYRAMIDS OF GIZA

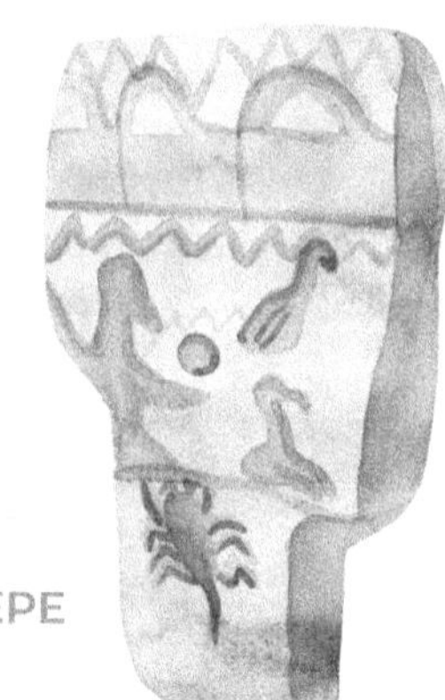

GÖBEKLI TEPE

ATHENA GODDESS OF WISDOM

Hermes Trismegestus

Hermes Trismegistus is the Greek name given to the Egyptian god Thoth. Hermes can also be found in both Islamic and Bahá'í writings associated with the prophet Idris. Master of philosophy, alchemy, and astrology, the ideas attributed to Hermes influenced the works of Pythagoras, Plato, Isaac Newton, Carl Jung, and many others.

Hermes Trismegestus   9500–8000 BCE

The **Vedas** are a collection of religious texts that originated in ancient India between 1500-900 BCE, which inform the beliefs and practices of Hinduism. The chariot is a metaphor for the Vedic model of the mind as expressed in the Katha Upanishad, Part I, Canto III, verse 3.

Our human experience is compared to a chariot representing the body, being pulled in many directions by five powerful horses which represent our senses. The driver is the intellect that holds the reins, representing the mind. The passenger and master of the chariot represents our true self.

"By thinking good thoughts, saying good words, and doing good deeds we become co-creators of our world."

Zoroaster, also known as Zarathustra, is regarded as the spiritual founder of Zoroastrianism. There is no scholarly consensus on when he lived, but it is estimated to be somewhere between 2000–500 BC. Zoroaster sees the human condition as a mental struggle between good and evil.

Zoroaster

Generally considered the founder of Taoism, **Lao Tzu,** also known as Laozi, wrote the Tao Te Ching in which the Tao, *the Way,* is taught through paradox and analogy. The Tao encourages surrender, simplicity, peace, and the disillusionment of the ego.

Lao Tzu

Buddha attained enlightenment by liberating his mind of saṅkhāra (conditioned things) and achieving dhyāna (concentration of mind). Through enlightenment, he attained three knowledges or insights into:

* His past lives
* The workings of Karma and Reincarnation
* The Four Noble Truths

Gaining insight into the Four Noble Truths is referred to as *awakening,* or nirvana, and signifies the cessation of desire and craving and, therefore, the end of suffering.

Gautama Buddha

Lao Tzu   6th century BCE

Gautama Buddha   6th–5th century BCE

Aristotle

Aristotle, a philosopher and polymath of Ancient Greece, produced the earliest known formal study of logic. He believed that reality could be best understood through empiricism— that is, observation and experience through the senses. In addition to the five senses, Aristotle recognized the existence of mental faculties, notably imagination and memory, that he called "inner senses." He believed the best way to understand why things are tthe way they are is to understand what purpose they serve.

René Descartes

René Descartes, a French mathematician, scientist, and philosopher, played a seminal role in the development of modern philosophy and science. He formulated the first modern version of mind-body dualism, asserting that the mind and body are separate, distinct entities composed of contrasting substances. Descartes championed a scientific approach grounded in observation and experimentation.

Aristotle 384–322 BCE

René Descartes 1596–1650

Ada Lovelace

Ada Lovelace, an English mathematician and writer, is credited as the world's first computer programmer. In the 1840s, she created programs for the yet-to-be-built Analytical Engine and was the first to propose that computers could move beyond calculation into symbolic and creative work—that numbers might stand for music, language, or ideas. Fascinated by the mind, she also envisioned a mathematical model of how thoughts and feelings arise—*"a calculus of the nervous system."* Though never realized, her insight foreshadowed modern concepts of computation and consciousness.

Often referred to as the father of American psychology, **William James** was a philosopher, historian, and psychologist. His work had a major influence on the development of American psychology and he was the first educator to teach a psychology course in the United States. He believed the mind, its experiences, and our nature are inseparable and described the mind as a "stream of consciousness."

William James

Sigmund Freud

An Austrian neurologist, **Sigmund Freud** founded a clinical method known as psychoanalysis—the practice by which psychopathologies are evaluated and treated through dialogue. The concept of the unconscious was central to Freud's theory of the mind. To describe the interactions and activities of the mind, he developed a model of psychic structure consisting of the id, ego, and super-ego. The id is the instinctual component of personality, responsible for emotional impulses and desires, particularly aggression and the sex drive. The ego seeks to please the id's desires in a realistic way, like a rider on a race horse. The super-ego compels us to follow the rules and norms imposed by our parents, our culture, and our education. The super-ego controls our sense of right and wrong, guilt and shame, and is our constant inner critic.

ID
INSTINCT

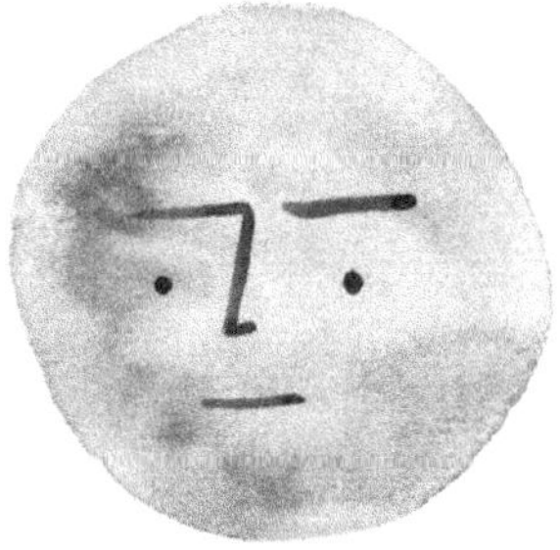

EGO
REALITY

SUPER-EGO
MORALITY

Sigmund Freud   1856–1939

Carl Jung was a Swiss psychiatrist and psychoanalyst who founded analytical psychology. In addition to being a practicing clinician and writer, Jung spent much of his time investigating the realms of philosophy and spirituality. He aimed to link the philosophical branch of epistemology (the theory of knowledge) with modern theories of psychology.

While investigating symbols that are shared across cultures and time, and are present in disparate religious, mythological, and magical systems, Jung arrived at the conclusion that the unconscious human psyche comprises two layers: the personal and collective unconscious. The personal unconscious consists of experiences that may have been forgotten or repressed yet still influence a person on an unconscious level. The collective unconscious accounts for the shared symbolisms that are present across the world throughout history, which hold memory traces common to all humans.

Carl Gustav Jung

PERSONAL UNCONSCIOUS

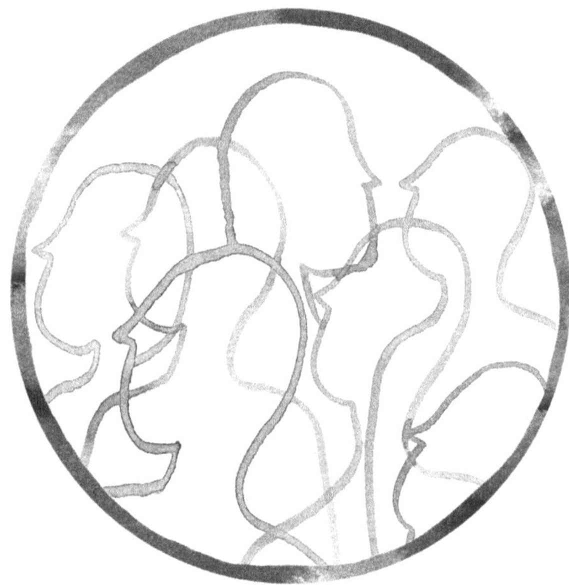

COLLECTIVE UNCONSCIOUS

Carl Gustav Jung   1875–1961

Jung believed that ancestral memories are passed on through *archetypes* that connect us to all humankind since the dawn of time. Archetypes are events such as birth and death, figures like the hero or the trickster, and motifs including the creation of the world or the apocalypse, that generate common imagery across all of humanity.

He described the archetypal world as "a residual sea of symbols, which is shared by all mankind, usually accessed through dreams or altered states, and from which cultures draw images on which to found their religions."[14]

ARCHETYPES

Jung felt these symbols originated from humanity itself throughout our shared history. He felt that each culture leaves behind impressions of its most sacred symbols, fueled by emotion or devotion to its gods and living mythology.

After the culture is long gone, these archetypal images remain dormant but may be revived simply by intending to connect, usually through visual imagery, as if through a universal picture language.

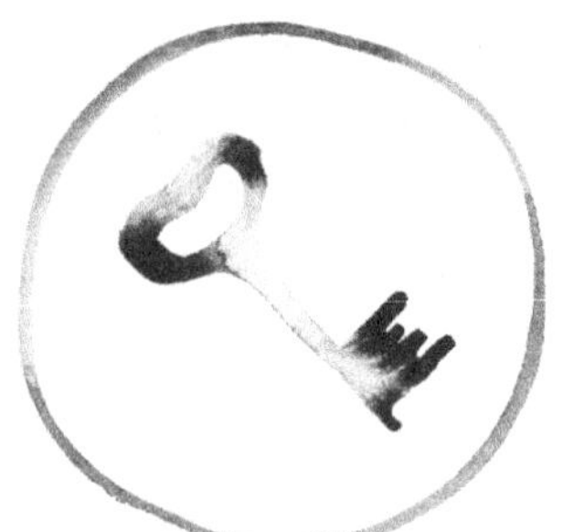

ARCHETYPE

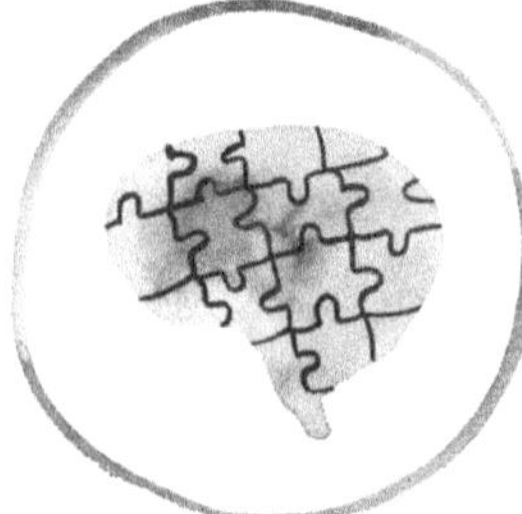

COLLECTIVE UNCONSCIOUS

COMPLEX

EXTRAVERSION & INTROVERSION

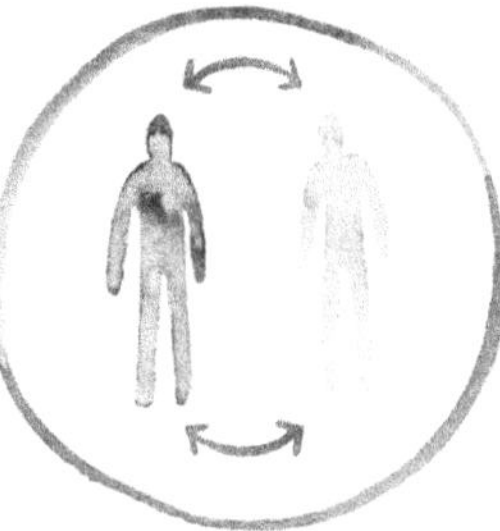

INDIVIDUATION

PERSONA

SYNCHRONICITY

Carl Jung is responsible for creating many key concepts commonly used today.

* **Archetype:** Universal themes and images shared across humanity.

* **Collective unconscious:** A sort of "species memory" shared across all cultures. The source of archetypes.

* **Complex subpersonality:** Collections of emotions, memories, perceptions, and desires that form around a common theme. These complexes can influence a person's thoughts and behaviors unconsciously.

* **Extraversion and introversion:** Personality traits that describe how open or reserved someone is, typically in relation to their social involvement.

* **Individuation:** A process of self-awareness and actualization through the integration of unconscious elements like the shadow.

* **Persona:** Subpersonalities, or social masks, that arise out of the desire to impress others while concealing aspects of our true selves.

* **Synchronicity:** A concept to describe experiences that appear meaningfully connected yet lack a causal connection, such as when you think of someone, and they call you moments later.

Virginia Satir was a family therapist who developed influential theories on communication, self-esteem, and relationships within family systems.

She believed that mental health and personal growth were deeply connected to family dynamics and communication patterns.

Virginia Satir

Mamie Phipps Clark

Mamie Phipps Clark was an American social psychologist, who was instrumental in studying the effects of racism on children's self-perception and mental health. Her research, particularly the famous "Doll Study," showed that African American children preferred white dolls over black dolls, revealing internalized racism and low self-esteem among children of color. Her research was used as evidence in the landmark Brown v. Board of Education Supreme Court case, which ruled that racial segregation in public schools was unconstitutional. Clark's work highlighted the deep psychological impact of racism and was pivotal in both social psychology and the civil rights movement, showing how social conditions influence the mind and identity.

Mamie Phipps Clark   1917–1983   *Virginia Satir   1916–1988*

Dame Jane Morris Goodall

An English primatologist, anthropologist, and activist, **Jane Goodall** is best known for her 60+ year study of chimpanzees. She observed human-like behaviors in chimpanzees, including armed conflict, tool usage, and sign language, suggesting more similarities to the human mind than genes alone might account for.

We should heed Goodall's observation that "Unfortunately, when there is a disconnect between mind and heart, technology can be, has been, and is being used for evil purposes. Unless our intellect is bonded closely with our feelings of love and compassion, although we may still be very clever, we shall not be wise."[15]

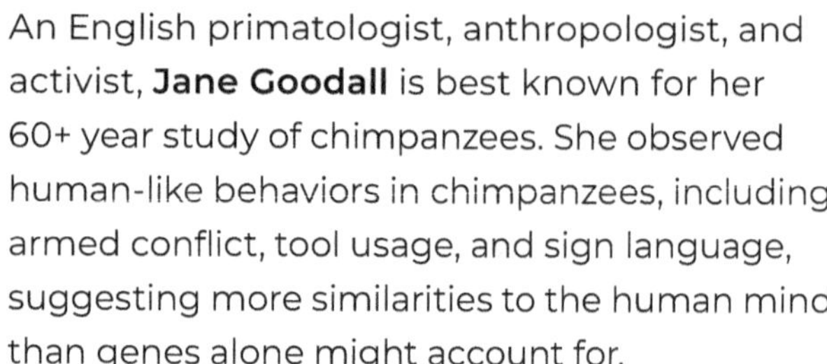

Lynne McTaggart

Lynne McTaggart, an investigative journalist and author, explores consciousness as a non-local phenomenon that interacts with a quantum field of energy. In books like *The Field* and *The Intention Experiment*, she challenges the materialist view, proposing that human intention can influence reality. Her work bridges quantum physics and neuroscience, suggesting the mind extends beyond the brain, reshaping ideas about human potential and interconnectedness.

Dame Jane Morris Goodall   1934-2025   *Lynne McTaggart   1951-Present*

Many unexplored chapters that could shed light on the evolution of the human mind, dating back thousands of years remain unwritten—leaving us with more questions than answers. For example, what role did lost cultures play in shaping our understanding of the mind? History, after all, is written by those in power. I want to honor the undocumented people who supported, inspired, and contributed to our understanding of the mind, yet whose voices have been forgotten.

 *Phew! With a long history like that, clearly the mind is a complex topic. Let's look to nature to help us envision the mind.*

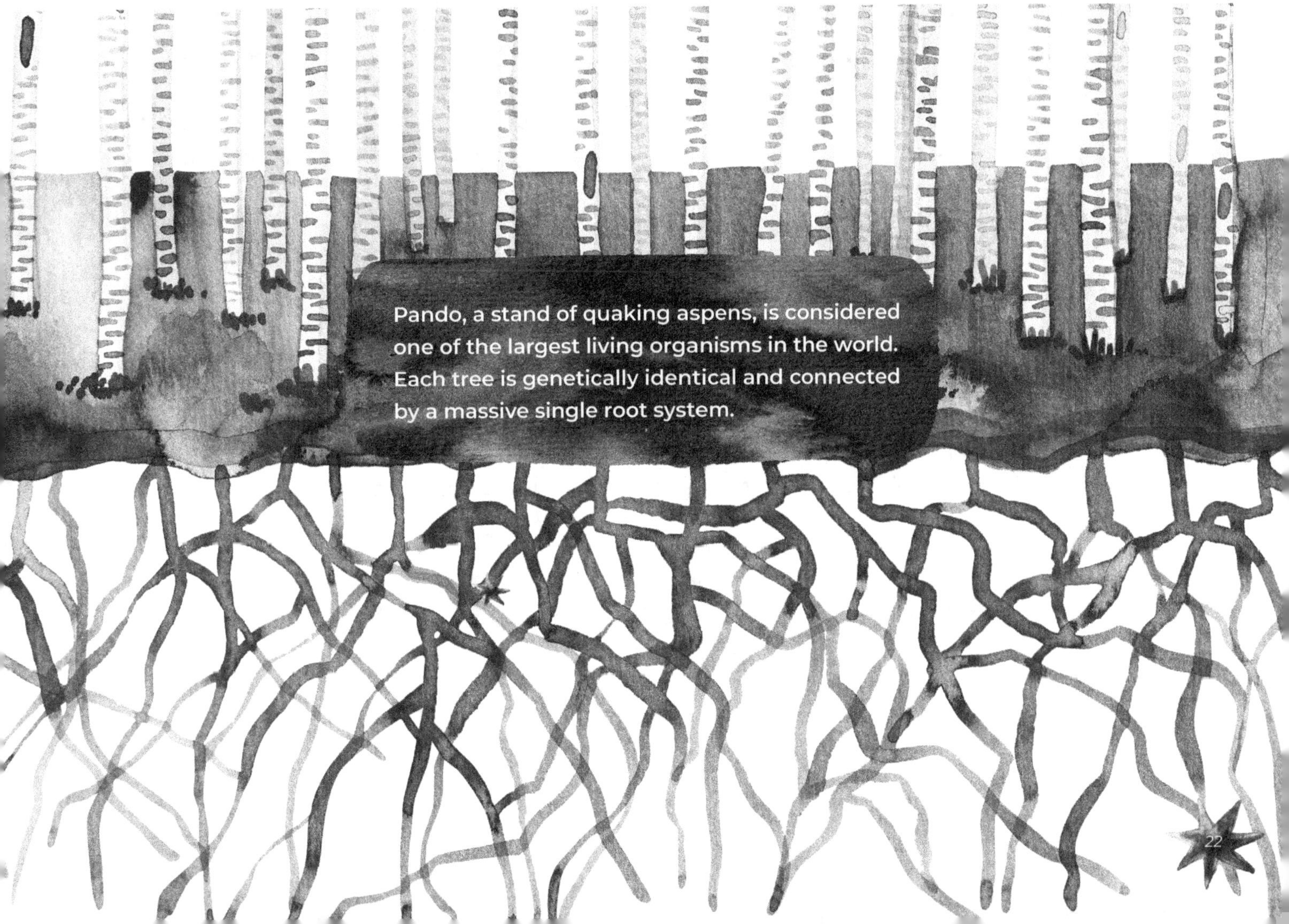

Pando, a stand of quaking aspens, is considered one of the largest living organisms in the world. Each tree is genetically identical and connected by a massive single root system.

Hardware

Billions of dollars have been poured into projects aimed at reverse engineering the brain.[16]

Despite advances in neuroscience, the fact that scientists still can't fully link mental processes to specific brain functions confirms the assertion by Michio Kaku that "What's sitting on your shoulders is the most complicated object in the known universe."[17]

The nervous system is responsible for (almost) the entirety of our experience of the world from the moment we're born. This is a pretty big deal— the biggest of deals, one might say.

Being educated on such an essential part of our existence would greatly empower us, yet most of us have only a vague idea how our nervous system works behind the scenes.

The nervous system can be likened to a supercomputer with central information processing areas and a variety of ports that communicate through intricate networks. This allows us to receive information and generate responses to it in real time.

Okay, so if the nervous system is responsible for our life experience, you might be wondering what our experience of life actually consists of.

Although the nervous system has many functions, the primary ones are:

* **Sensation:** We decode what happens in our environment with our sensory receptors, detecting light photons through our eyes, sound waves through our ears, and chemicals through our noses. We experience taste with the chemical receptors on our tongues, and touch and pain with the receptors on our skin. These signals run along bundles of sensory nerves to the spinal cord to the brain, where they are interpreted.

* **Perception:** Our nervous system interprets sensory information by focusing on certain details while filtering out others. Perception, closely linked to attention, acts like the spotlight of our awareness. It determines what stands out in our experience and what fades into the background. For instance, we constantly receive sensory input—like the pressure of our feet on the ground—but it only enters our awareness when we consciously tune in to it.

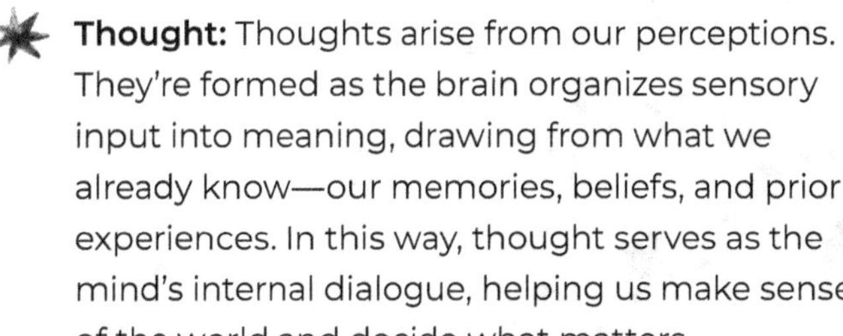

* **Thought:** Thoughts arise from our perceptions. They're formed as the brain organizes sensory input into meaning, drawing from what we already know—our memories, beliefs, and prior experiences. In this way, thought serves as the mind's internal dialogue, helping us make sense of the world and decide what matters.

* **Response:** Generated by neurons in our brain, our responses to the information our brain processes help us to stay alive (running from a perceived threat) and maintain homeostasis, aka balance (returning to calm once the threat has passed). Responses can be either automatic or voluntary. Breathing is a good example of physical behavior that can be either: it happens automatically, but we can have voluntary motor control over our breathing if we direct our attention to the way we breathe.

Thoughts can also be voluntary or automatic!

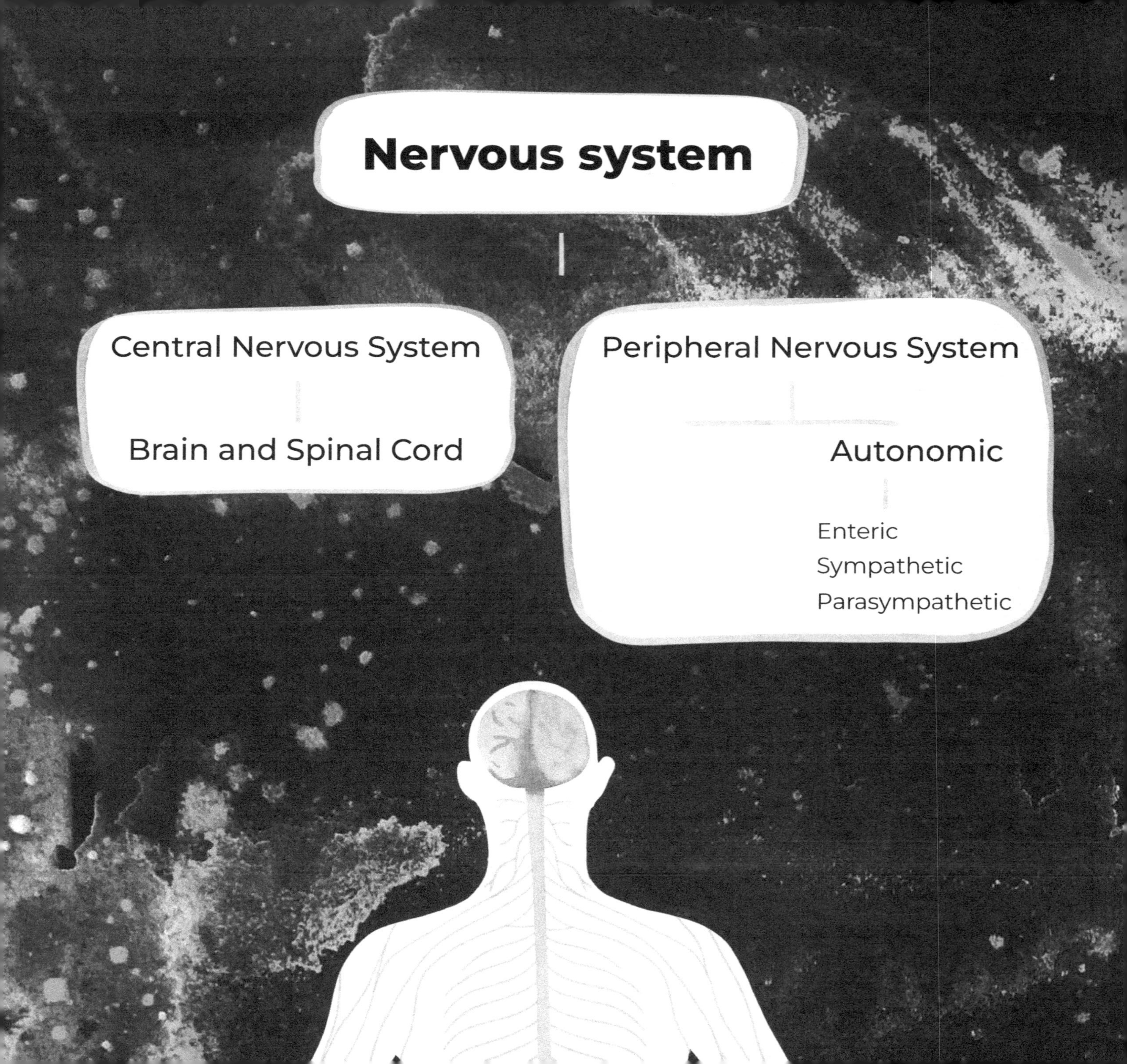

Nervous system
Central Nervous System
Brain and Spinal Cord
Peripheral Nervous System
Autonomic
Enteric
Sympathetic
Parasympathetic

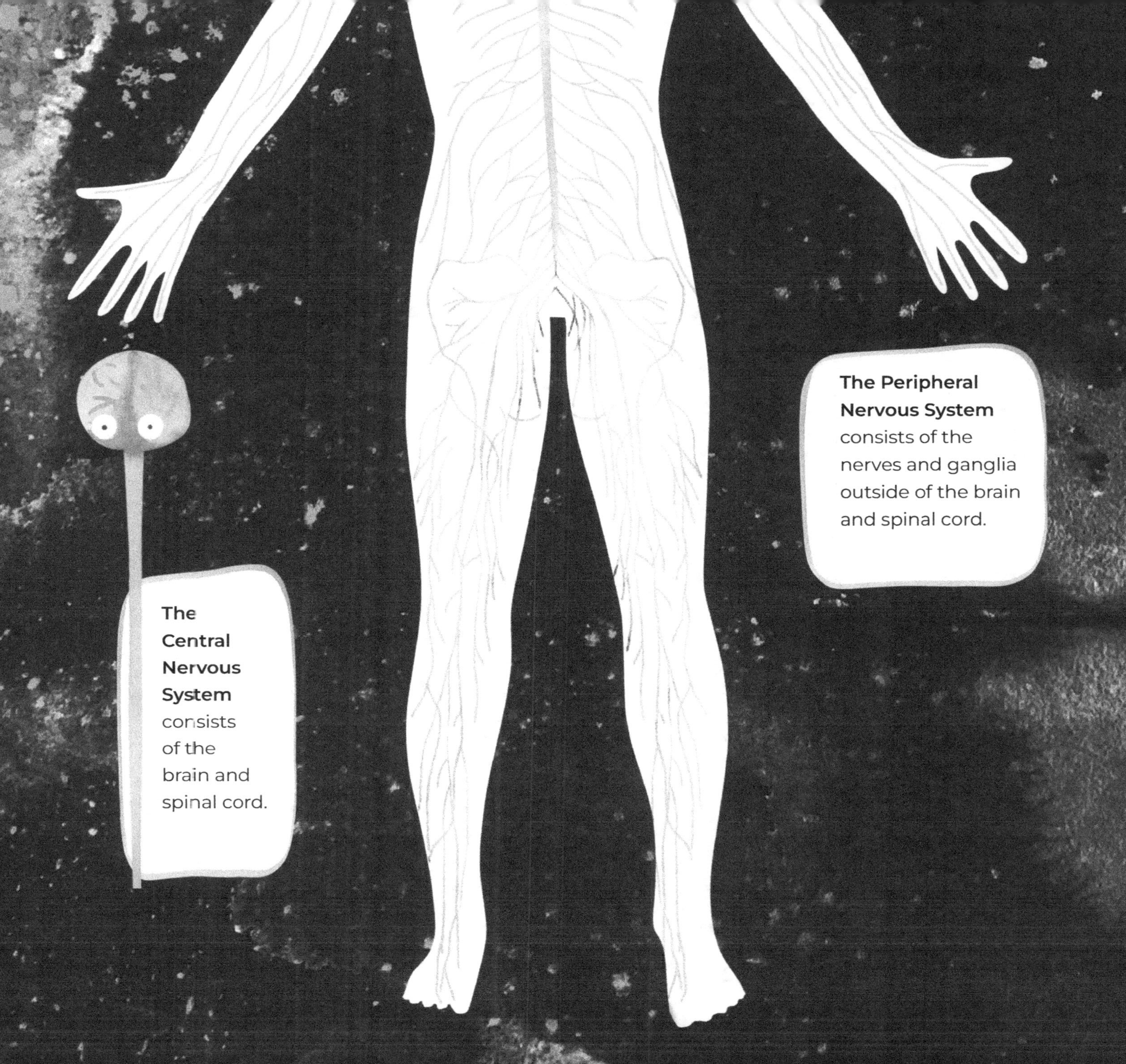

The Peripheral Nervous System consists of the nerves and ganglia outside of the brain and spinal cord.
The Central Nervous System consists of the brain and spinal cord.

Central Nervous System and Brain

The nervous system consists of two main subsystems: the **central nervous system,** which consists of the brain and spinal cord, and the **peripheral nervous system** that comprises the nerves and ganglia outside the brain and spinal cord.

The **brain** is the CEO of the nervous system and oversees almost every major body system. It has 86 billion glucose-gobbling **neurons,** or brain cells, that communicate through an amazing electrochemical process called synaptic transmission.

THE NEURON'S STRUCTURE:

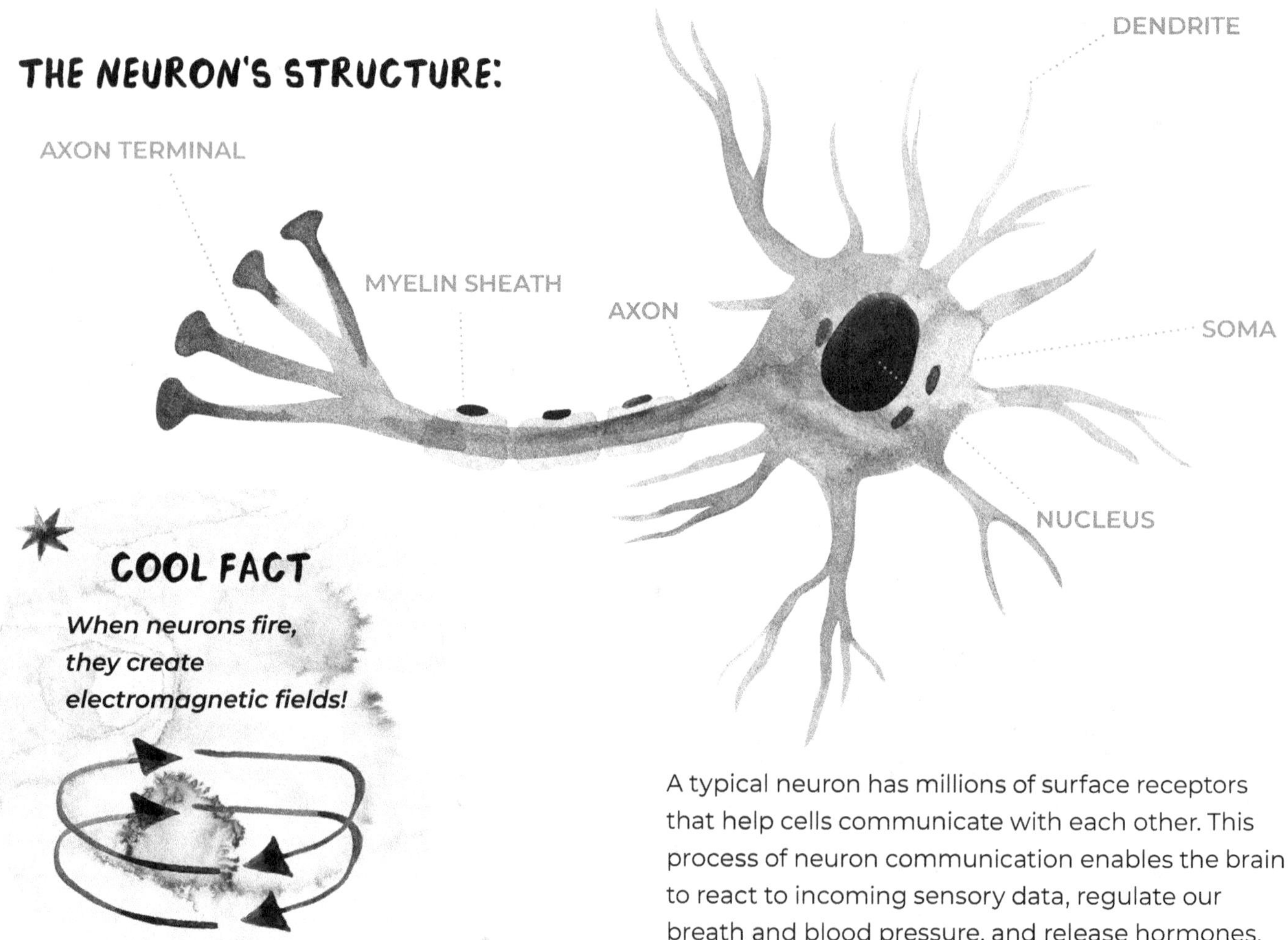

COOL FACT

When neurons fire, they create electromagnetic fields!

A typical neuron has millions of surface receptors that help cells communicate with each other. This process of neuron communication enables the brain to react to incoming sensory data, regulate our breath and blood pressure, and release hormones.

The largest part of the brain, the **cerebrum,** has two hemispheres, each containing four lobes that process different types of information.

Let's review some of the functions of each lobe. Please note that these functions are somewhat oversimplified, since most activities require the coordination of several lobes in both hemispheres.

The **frontal lobe** plays a role in focus, planning, reasoning, problem-solving, and emotional regulation. Damage to the frontal lobe can cause changes in someone's personality and social behavior. The frontal lobe can silence our inner critic.

The **parietal lobe** is responsible for touch, pain, temperature, spatial perception, and body orientation.

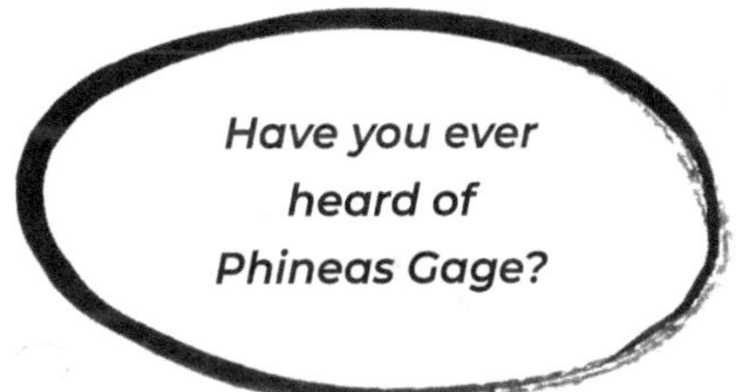

The **temporal lobe** is involved in learning, memory, smell, hearing, and recognizing complex visual information such as faces and scenes.

The **occipital lobe** is the main area involved with sight. It contains the primary visual cortex, which receives information from the eyes and relays it to secondary visual processing areas that interpret the depth, distance, location, and identity of seen objects.

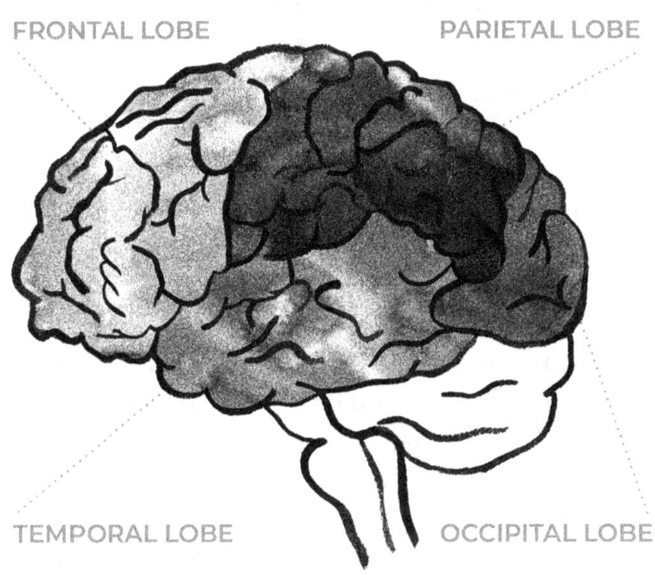

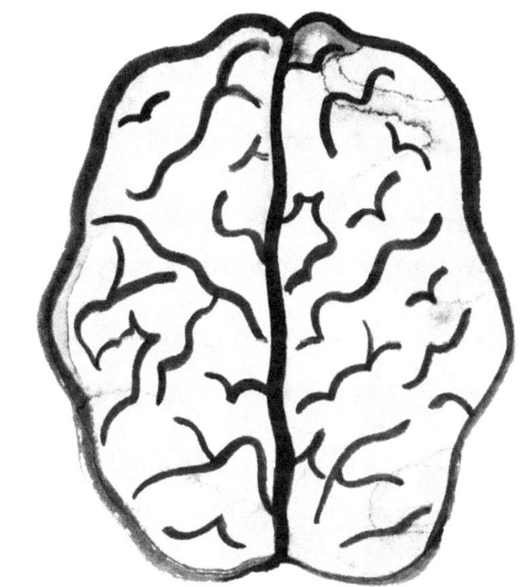

Peripheral Nervous System

The **peripheral nervous system** links the central nervous system with the rest of the body. The peripheral nervous system can be further subdivided into the **somatic nervous system** and the **autonomic nervous system.**

Stemming from the Greek word *soma*, meaning body, the somatic nervous system is responsible for relaying sensory and motor information to and from the central nervous system. The somatic nervous system contains two major types of neurons: **motor neurons,** which carry information from the central nervous system to the muscles, allowing for voluntary movement, and **sensory neurons,** which send sensory information, such as touch, to the brain and spinal cord for interpretation.

The **autonomic nervous system (ANS)** regulates the body's involuntary functions, like blood flow, heart rate, digestion, and breathing.

The ANS has three subsystems: the **enteric nervous system,** the **sympathetic nervous system,** and the **parasympathetic nervous system.**

Often referred to as the *second brain*, the enteric nervous system forms one half of the brain-gut connection. While its main function is to control digestion, it also produces 50% of our dopamine— the neurotransmitter involved in pleasure, motivation, and learning.

This bidirectional communication is facilitated by the **vagus nerve,** linking the gut and brain in constant dialogue.

Perhaps you've heard of the **"fight-or-flight"** response, which is the primary function regulated by the sympathetic nervous system. This function prepares our body to expend energy in response to an external threat by heightening our senses.

The stress response produces increased heart and breathing rates, increased blood flow to the muscles, dilation of the pupils, and an activation of the sweat glands. This heightened state of awareness changes our perception of time increasing our "frames per second," so to speak, in order to help us make quick survival-based decisions.

On the flip side is the parasympathetic nervous system that helps regulate normal bodily functions and brings the body back to the resting state.

Sometimes referred to as the **"rest and digest"** state, the goal of the parasympathetic nervous system
is to conserve energy and reduce breathing, heart rate, and blood flow to the muscles. Hello, food coma!

All of this information might sound a bit technical, but the important point to take away is that the nervous system is involved in nearly everything you experience.

Furthermore, people often consider emotions and thoughts to be conceptual or non-physical, but they act upon the hardware of our nervous system, causing very real biochemical changes in the body.

These changes affect our health, mood, energy levels, and even our cognitive abilities. When our bodies spend too much energy dealing with stress—a function of the sympathetic nervous system—and emotions are not expressed and released, the body and mind can eventually fall victim to illness and disease.

As we move into the next section, you'll learn how the mind and our thoughts have the power to shape not only our physical and mental well-being but the entire trajectory of our lives as well.

As a hypnotist, I've been privileged to work with clients whose stories have stayed with me. One of my favorites is the story of a woman I'll call Bev…

One day, Bev stepped into my office—a poised foreign diplomat visiting the United States. Her calm exterior briefly masked a swirl of emotion, yet her slumped posture told a different story: quiet defeat shadowed her presence.

As we started to talk, her emotional pain surfaced. The storm brewing in Bev's life seemed deceptively straightforward—her grown daughter's wish to meet her birth father. Yet, the backstory carried significant weight. This man had abandoned Bev during her pregnancy, leaving deep, enduring scars.

During her account of the situation, she frequently used terms like "this is killing me" and "I'm dying inside." Language like this is a flag because it signals a subconscious clue as to where the story will lead.

Her reaction to the upcoming meeting seemed exaggerated to her family and friends, yet the profound pain and anguish she felt were genuine. The weight of the past bore heavily upon her, refusing to be shrugged off.

During our first session, I brought Bev into a hypnotic state. She unexpectedly and spontaneously regressed to a past life where she lived in the countryside of England.

In this vivid reverie, she recalled her thatched cottage, wooden furniture, and her simple attire. She had been a midwife, and her reputation as a skillful herbalist ultimately led to some of the villagers branding her a witch.

After witch hunters broke down her door, the soldiers who accompanied them barged in to arrest her, and one particularly ferocious individual killed her in her own home. As she recalled her horrific death, Bev moaned and emanated shock and anguish.

After a thorough emotional release process she experienced a compelling understanding of the scene and its context.

It turned out that the soldier who killed her was the very man who had abandoned her during her pregnancy in this current lifetime.

She felt greatly relieved after the session, both of us believing she had solved the puzzle as to why she had been so emotionally affected by this man.

A week later, Bev returned to my office for her follow-up session. I intended to reinforce the positive suggestions I had given her and to fortify the progress she had made with a fun mind training session.

As we neared the end of the session, I encouraged her to practice self-care, telling her to "treat herself like a queen." A moment later, she gave a cry as if she had received an unexpected blow. Despite my confusion (and concern for the client in my waiting room) it was clear we had more work to do.

Tears welled up, and she shared graphic details of a different time and place that turned out to be another chapter of her soul's incredible journey.

In this alternate existence, Bev was a royal figure, deeply in love with a servant who worked in her father's castle. She became pregnant. Unfortunately, her noble obligations mandated that she marry into another family to cement a political alliance. Together, she and her love concocted an escape plan, but on the night they were to flee, she failed to show up. Bev abandoned her lover eventually raising their child with another man, and never knew what became of him.

As we processed the meaning of this new revelation, the pieces of this multi-lifetime puzzle seemed to come together. With her newfound insights, Bev felt deep regret for the pain she must have put him through.

I led Bev through the healing process, and it was clear she wanted to forgive herself as well as this man. Upon releasing the emotions and achieving understanding, she realized that the origin of the betrayal started well before she had imagined.

Our session allowed Bev to let go of the guilt she carried for hurting her lover in that past life, a burden she had unknowingly carried through vast expanses of time. Her posture and facial expression transformed, and she exuded strength, peace, and confidence. She left that room with clarity of mind, and without the emotional charge she felt previously when thinking of her daughter meeting her father. Her perspective had transformed, replacing bitterness with compassion. Bev could accept her role in hurting her lover and, in turn, his role in hurting her—they both played a part in the unfolding of their story.

The implications were immediately clear to me as these interwoven stories left me in awe—each thread a revelation. Those sessions changed my perspective about karma and the labels of villain and victim that are often too easily assigned to the people who are involved in emotionally painful situations.

This story is a testament to the transformative potential of understanding and empathy, highlighting the power of revisiting the past and reframing our beliefs. When we encounter such past-life memories, I tell my clients that it makes no difference if these experiences are real or imagined. The subconscious mind finds resolution through stories, so we can take the relief we get—and build upon it.

Software

The Conscious Mind

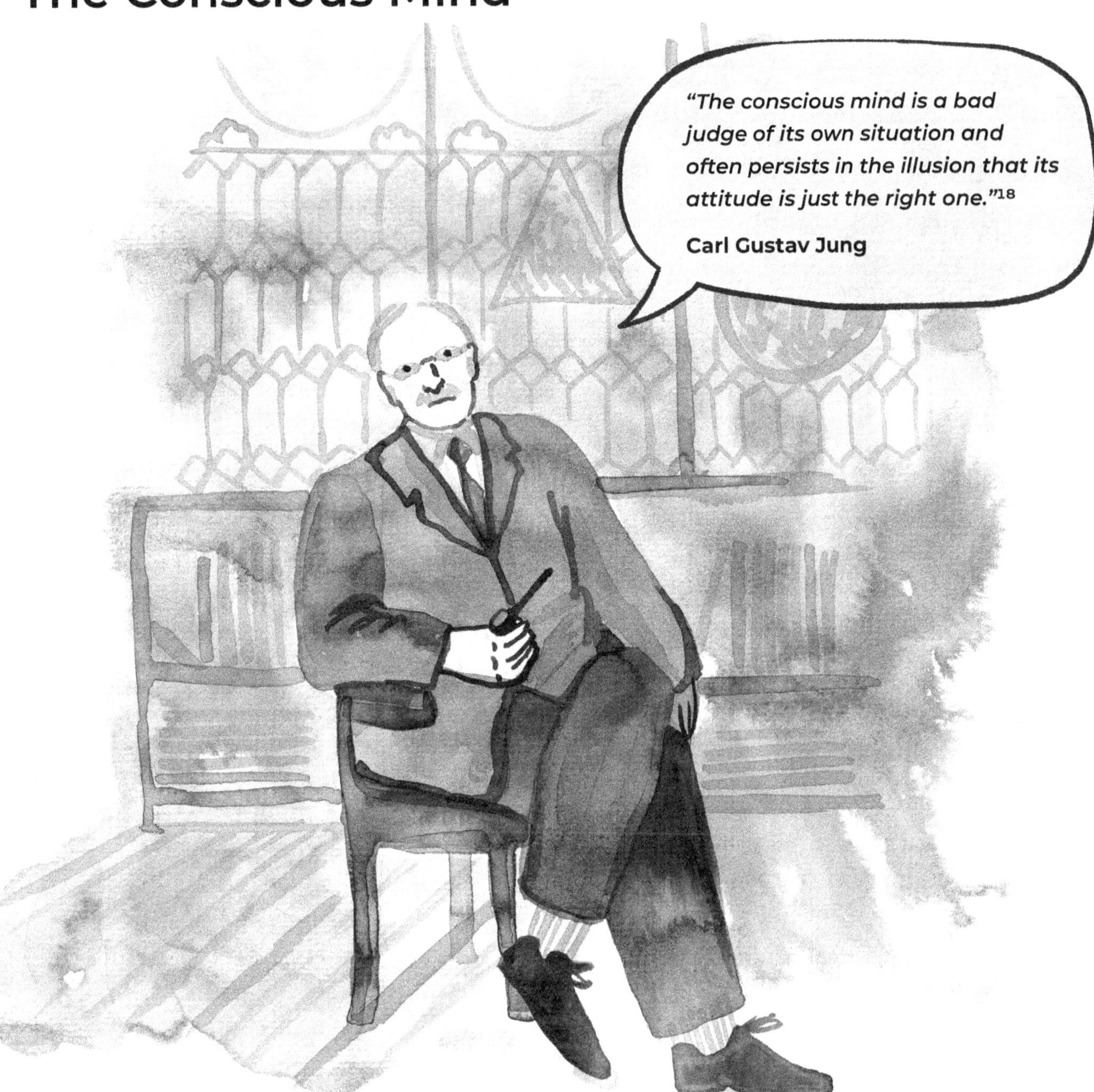

THE CONSCIOUS MIND'S FUNCTIONS:

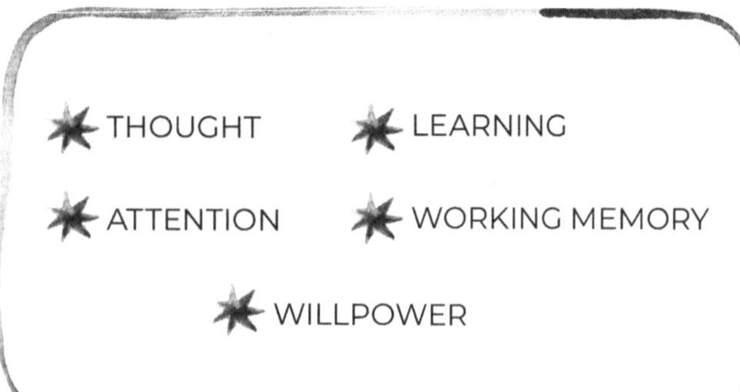

The conscious mind comprises key functions that form the foundation of our awareness, decisions and actions. These include: thought, attention, learning, working memory and willpower.

Not to be confused with the umbrella term consciousness, which refers to awareness more generally, the conscious mind is typically what we experience as "ourselves." It includes our awareness of the present moment, as well as our thoughts and the information stored in our short-term memory.

Even though the conscious mind is limited in scope, it is incredibly good at steering the subconscious mind and the body.

PREFRONTAL CORTEX

The rule-making, self-aware part of the brain most related to the conscious mind is the prefrontal cortex (PFC).

The PFC helps us operate in different situations and is linked to executive functions such as decision-making, planning, self-control, and problem-solving. It orchestrates thought and action according to our goals.

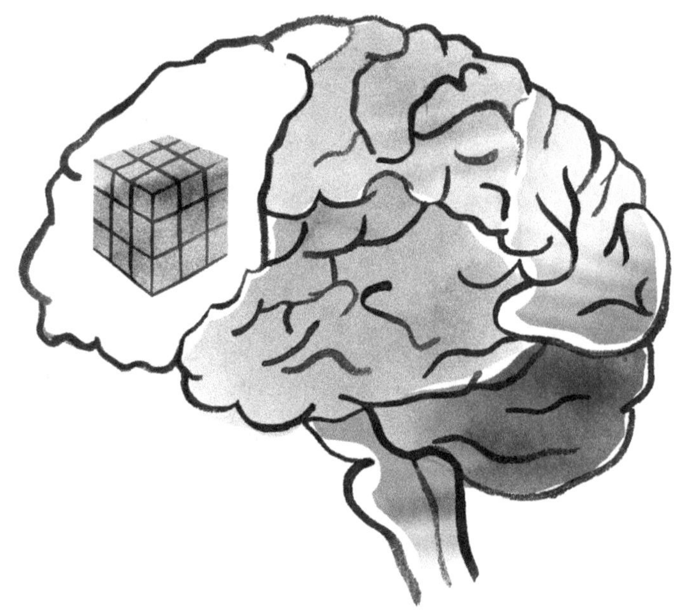

Thought

One could say that thought, or thinking, is the foundation of the conscious mind. It allows us to make a model of the world and respond to it according to our goals and desires.

Thoughts are representations of things, similar to how a drawing of a tree represents, but is not the actual tree. However, thoughts do exist as physical entities in the brain—acting as representations of information, much like the drawing.

Information is not an abstract concept; it exists in the physical universe. Writing on paper or etchings on stone, binary data in computing, or stamps on your local cafe's loyalty card—all represent information. Thoughts are patterns of electrochemical information and cannot occur without their canvas, the neural substrate.

So, where do thoughts come from?
Subjectively, they seem to come from nowhere; they just pop into your head.

"Oh man, I'd love some ramen right now."

Objectively, however, they do actually come from somewhere. Thoughts arise from electrical signals generated by neurons, propagating through the brain in wave-like patterns. This process happens in response to our environment in the present moment. The sensory data we take in is then filtered through past experiences and memory.

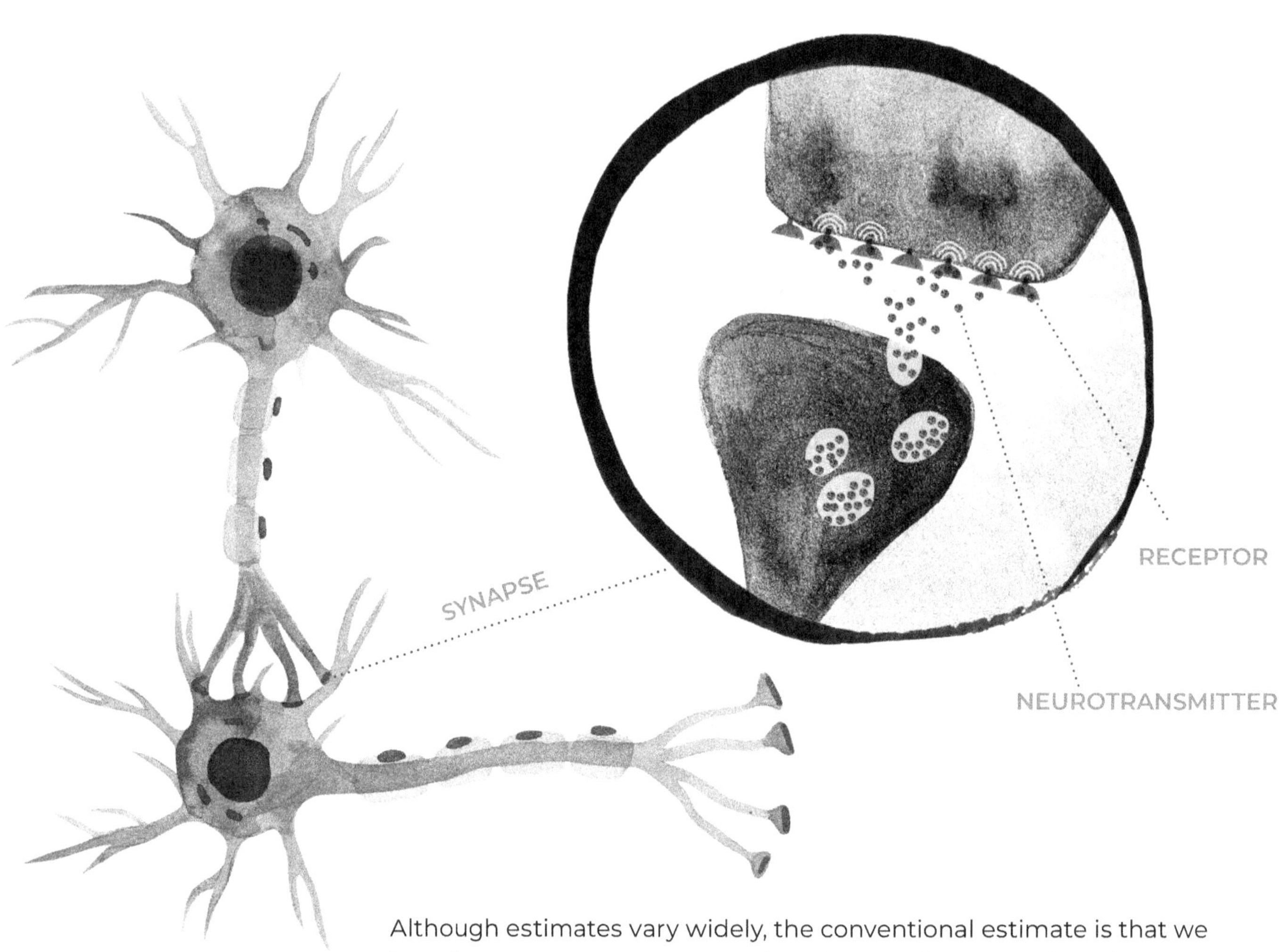

Although estimates vary widely, the conventional estimate is that we have between 5,000 to 60,000 thoughts per day. These thoughts are associative and usually come in a chain, with one idea leading to the next. Thoughts generally take the form of reasoning, analysis, or judgment.

We auto-suggest thoughts all day long without examining their content or tone. This self-talk slips past our conscious awareness and activates our nervous system.

The overwhelming majority of these thoughts are habitual, unoriginal, and unconscious: often arising in reaction to how we feel. A vicious cycle ensues when we surrender to thoughts and act upon them as if they were true.

The freedom to think our own thoughts and choose our attitudes toward the circumstances we find ourselves in, is the one thing every human being has complete control over. Yet ironically, most people put little effort into understanding or training this crucial ability.

With so many thoughts popping into our conscious experience, what really matters is the quality of our thoughts.

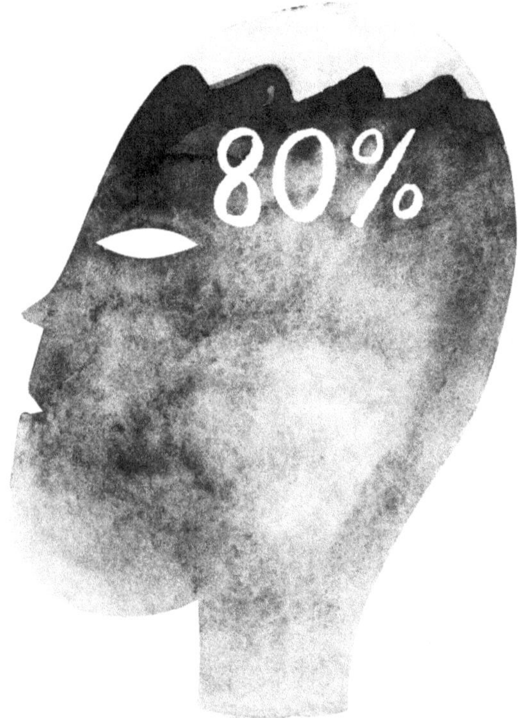

Approximately 80% of the average person's thoughts are negative.[22] [23] Just think about what that does to how we see ourselves, our lives, and the world around us. These negative thoughts stir up low-vibe emotions and distort reality, giving us a disheartened view of life and leading us to unconsciously generate our own suffering.

On the flip side, positive thinkers not only live about seven years longer than pessimists—they also enjoy a richer, more vibrant life with less pain. They're more open to suggestion, more responsive to uplifting ideas, and more likely to activate the powerful effects of placebo.

So, why are we so often negative?

It has everything to do with what we believe. To maintain homeostasis and reduce our cognitive load, our minds create beliefs in the form of prejudices, that are stored in the subconscious mind.

Even though these beliefs are generally beyond our everyday awareness, they still have a powerful effect on us. On this subject William James noted that "A great many people think they are thinking when they are merely rearranging their prejudices… We keep unaltered as many of our old prejudices and beliefs as we can. We patch and tinker more than we renew." [24]

This quote suggests that the human tendency is to cling to existing beliefs. We often resist change, making only minor adjustments instead of fully embracing new perspectives.

Beliefs are turbo-charged thoughts that we have accepted as truth. Once we form a belief, it becomes the template and engine of future thoughts. When we hold negative and untrue beliefs, they are like factories, generating related negative thoughts as we navigate our life experiences.

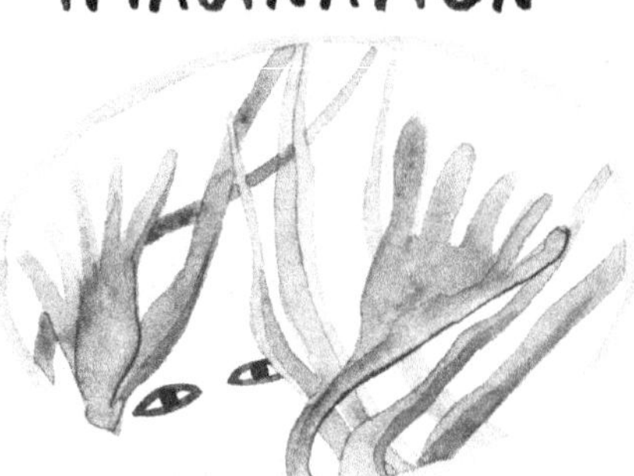

What might be possible if, before acting on a thought, we engaged our reason, imagination and conscience?

✴ **Reason:** evaluates thoughts by comparing them to one's past experiences stored in the memory, then forming judgments and opinions based on logic.

✴ **Imagination:** shapes thoughts and ideas into plans and possibilities.

✴ **Conscience:** provides moral guidance, ensuring our thoughts align with ethical principles.[25]

Taking a moment to assess our thoughts gives us the space in which to evaluate whether a thought is true and empowering or if it is the product of an untrue belief and should simply be released. The Buddhist monk, K. Sri Dhammananda, writes that we should be mindful of the way our thoughts shape our lives because "we are what we think. All that we are arises with our thoughts. With our thoughts we make the world."[26]

Accurate, organized thinking is the most important skill for success. We can use our thoughts systematically to form thought-habits for the greatest efficiency.

In the subconscious mind section, we'll explore beliefs in greater detail.

Attention

Who doesn't love a little attention?

If you aspire to upgrade your conscious mind, mastering your attention is a great place to start.

The job of the prefrontal cortex is to concentrate and keep the mind on track. The prefrontal cortex has been doing the heavy lifting while you've been reading this book.

You've probably also felt your attention being pulled in different directions while trying to focus on reading.

Your phone vibrates, and the screen lights up. You glance over to see who's messaging you.

Oh, it's your best friend sending a cat meme!

The meme reminds you that you forgot to feed your cat—who also probably tried to get your attention.

Next thing you know, you're cleaning the entire house as the book lies forgotten.

Finally, you come back to the book and find it nearly impossible to concentrate because now your thoughts are all over the place. Can you relate? Situations like these happen all the time. In this world of notification overload, it is no wonder that we struggle to focus our attention. The problem is that we cannot fight our monkey mind, which loves information; we can only re-direct it.

We are always using our attention, and that means that it must go somewhere. Rather than allowing it to be diluted or squandered, we can learn to harness and command it.

Focused attention is the ability to maintain concentration on a task or thought by effectively managing emotional and sensory distractions from our inner and outer environments. And like any skill, we can practice to improve it. Moreover, the ability to engage and disengage attention is vital for our overall well-being.

Before we go any further, we need to address the elephant in the room.

The one in the corner writing an essay while listening to a podcast and watching Netflix.

That elephant isn't real. And neither is **multitasking.**

In our culture of hustle and achievement, we've been taught that multitasking—in other words, doing several cognitive tasks at the same time—is a desirable, if not necessary, skill.

Unfortunately, our brains don't quite work like that. As with a TV or radio station, we can only tune

in to one at a time. What is really happening is **task switching.** Since our brains can't perform multiple tasks at the same time, we are constantly shifting our attention between tasks. Daniel Goleman explains that "what many people think of as 'splitting' attention in multitasking…is a fiction" because "rather than having a stretchable balloon of attention to deploy in tandem, we have a narrow, fixed pipeline to allot. Instead of splitting it, we actually switch rapidly. Continual switching saps attention from full, concentrated engagement."[28]

This act of rapidly switching tasks has a negative impact on our productivity and make us more prone to mistakes. The neuroscientist Daniel Levitin unequivocally states that "multitasking is the enemy of a focused attentional system. Increasingly, we demand that our attentional system try to focus on several things at once, something that it was not evolved to do."[29] Not only that, but our attempts to multitask can also impair short-term memory, increase anxiety and stress, inhibit creativity, and hinders our ability to enter *flow* states—where the real magic happens.

This is why the skill of focus is so important. By focusing on less, we can, ironically, achieve more.

When we are fully focused on something, the circuitry in our brain synchronizes with the stimulus it is tuned into, and everything else fades into the background. Time seems to disappear, and all other thoughts subside. This is the state I help my clients access during transformative sessions because it is a powerful state for learning.

When trying to focus our attention on a task, the way in which we set up our workspace matters. Objects in our environment are magnets for our attention, each subtly drawing a portion of our focus toward it. Whenever we clear something, we release its pull on our awareness, freeing up mental space and reclaiming our attention. Having a clean and minimal work environment can help us maintain our focus on the task at hand.

Attention is key to learning and memory and it helps us map information. Attention enriches our most well-used circuits and wires us to respond to new and potentially threatening situations. When we pay attention, a biochemical environment is produced that assists us in forming memories. Attention says, "Hey, this is important; let's remember this!"

Attention and perception are inherently linked.

While standing, we only perceive the pressure on our feet if we direct our attention to it. The same principle applies to our perception of pain.

Directing attention to pain in the body brings more pain into existence, because those circuits in the brain that perceive pain become electrically activated.

If we put attention elsewhere, brain circuits that process pain can be turned off, but when we look for the pain to see if it's still there, it comes rushing back. Paying attention to pain increases our sensitivity to it.

DID YOU KNOW...

Whispering in someone's right ear is more effective at getting their attention than in their left ear? Studies in neuroscience and psychology have found that people generally process verbal information more efficiently through their right ear, which is linked to the left hemisphere of the brain—often associated with language and logic processing. This phenomenon is known as the "right-ear advantage."

One notable study found that people were more likely to comply with requests made into their right ear, likely because information received through this side is more effectively processed and retained. This research supports the idea that, in situations where clear communication or persuasion is crucial, speaking into the right ear might be beneficial!

This principle also applies to our emotions and thoughts. When we direct our attention to negative thoughts, we activate our emotions in response. The longer we focus on fear-based thoughts, the more fear and anxiety we create. Most of us have had an experience of "spiraling," where we fixate on negative thinking and allow our stress to get progressively worse.

Stress takes us right out of creation mode and puts us into survival mode, where we pay more attention to problems, threats, and the outer world rather than to our inner, resourceful, creative mind.

The good news is that, by focusing our attention, we can train ourselves to shift the emphasis from unhelpful thoughts to positive, encouraging thoughts. We can therefore alter our emotional state and our perception of circumstances. With consistent awareness and redirection of our attention, it is possible to change our base state and see ourselves and the world through a more optimistic lens.

Understanding how our attention works and how to direct it efficiently is an immensely powerful tool. Most people don't realize how much time they waste each day by allowing their attention to be pulled all over the place. Mastering our attention not only enables us to accomplish more each day but also transforms how we experience the rich and ever-changing journey of life.

MENTAL FILTRATION SYSTEM

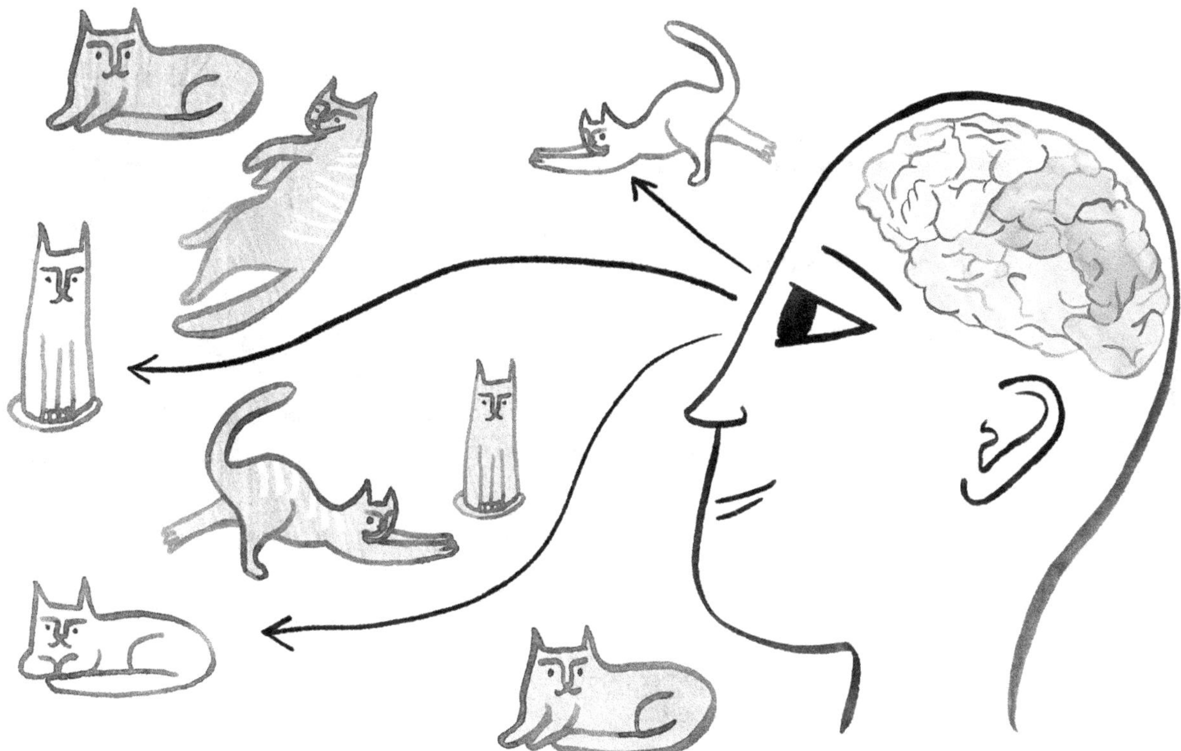

The **Reticular Activating System (RAS)** is a network of neurons located in your brainstem that filters out unnecessary information to make sure that the important stuff gets through.

Most of the time, It discards all but about one percent of the information in our environment based on what is currently relevant to us. For example: ever notice that when you have a certain type of car In mind, suddenly you start to notice that car everywhere?

That's not serendipity, but the RAS at work.

The RAS influences everything we think, say, and do. It plays an important role in focus, arousal, the fight-or-flight response, motivation and behavior. Our senses are wired directly to the RAS which filters sensory input and prioritizes our attention. It influences the central nervous system and seeks information that validates our beliefs, contributing to confirmation bias.

Fortunately, we can reset or adjust the RAS to better serve us by consistently shifting our focus.

Learning

Learning—acquiring knowledge and skills—is essential for changing our behavior. When we know better, we are empowered to do better.

However, learning is greatly limited without the ability to retain and recall information. It requires forming new synaptic connections and building neural networks. Remembering depends on effectively maintaining and strengthening these pathways.

The challenge is that we are forgetting machines—wired to forget more easily than to remember. If we don't actively reinforce what we've learned, the new neural pathways formed during periods of focused attention can fade quickly, sometimes within hours. The brain, in its drive for efficiency, prunes away these connections unless they are deemed important.

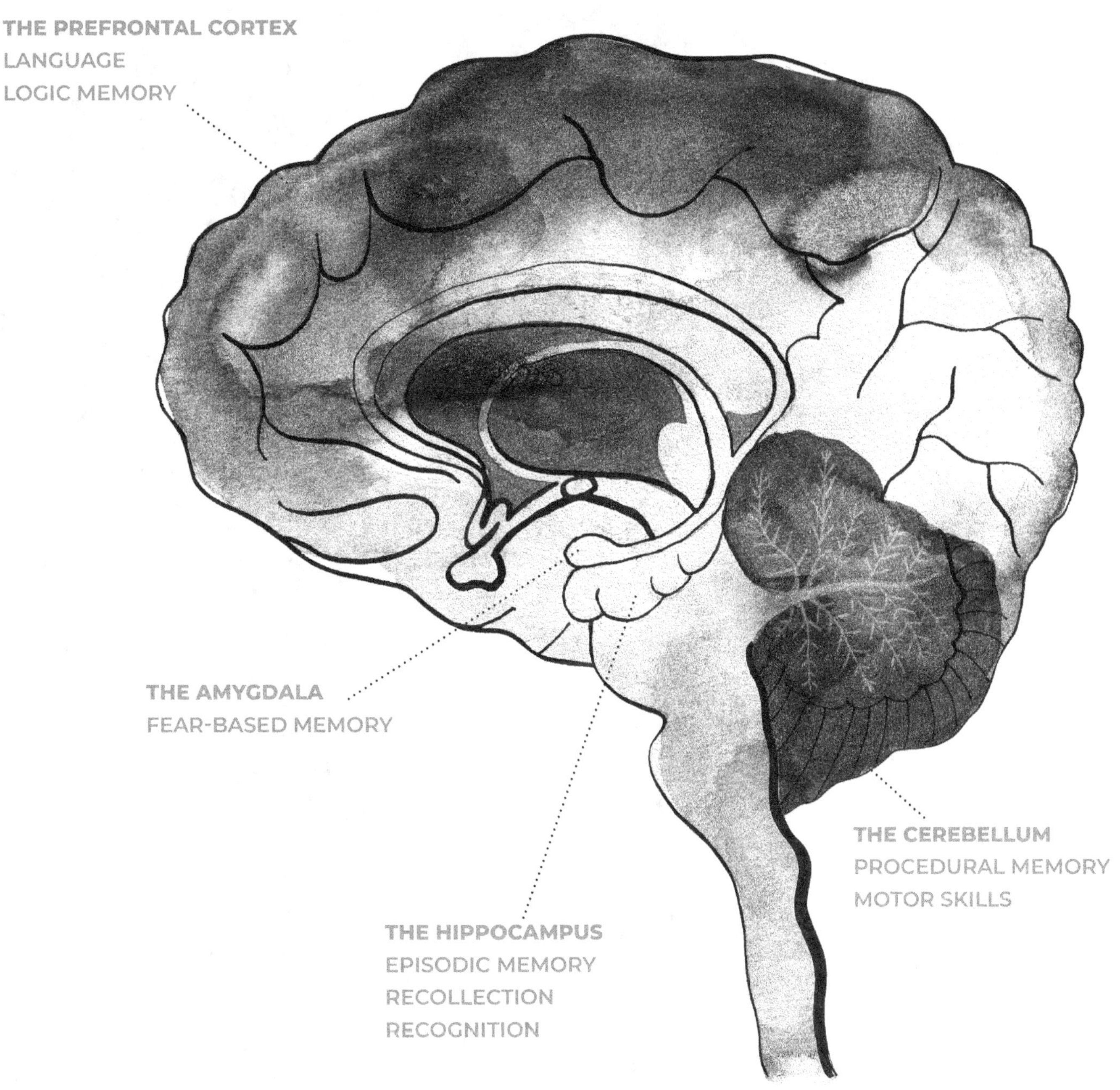

THE PREFRONTAL CORTEX
LANGUAGE
LOGIC MEMORY

THE AMYGDALA
FEAR-BASED MEMORY

THE CEREBELLUM
PROCEDURAL MEMORY
MOTOR SKILLS

THE HIPPOCAMPUS
EPISODIC MEMORY
RECOLLECTION
RECOGNITION

The brain has an estimated
quadrillion synaptic connections.
That's about ten thousand times
more than the number of stars
in the Milky Way Galaxy—
roughly one hundred billion.

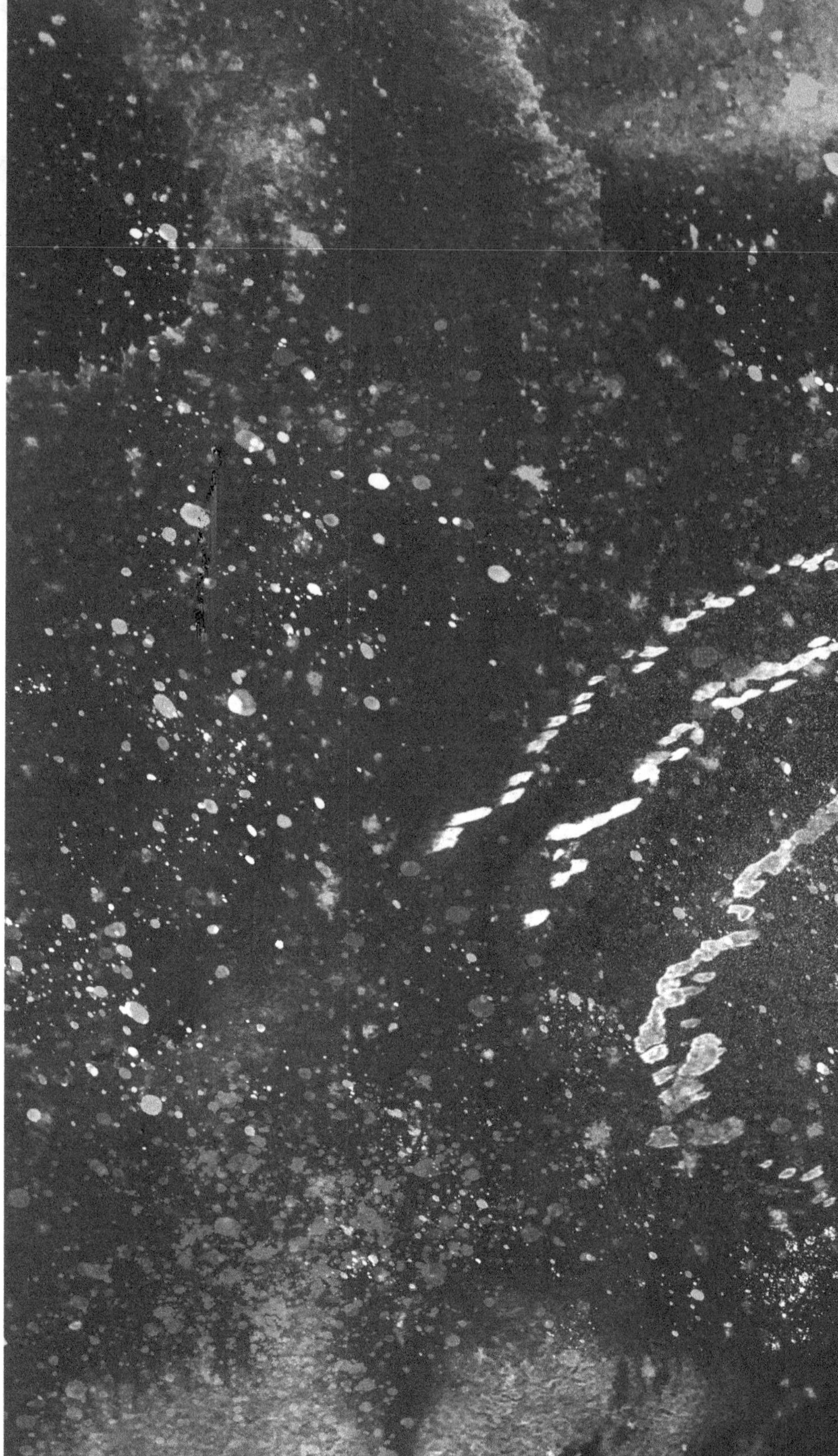

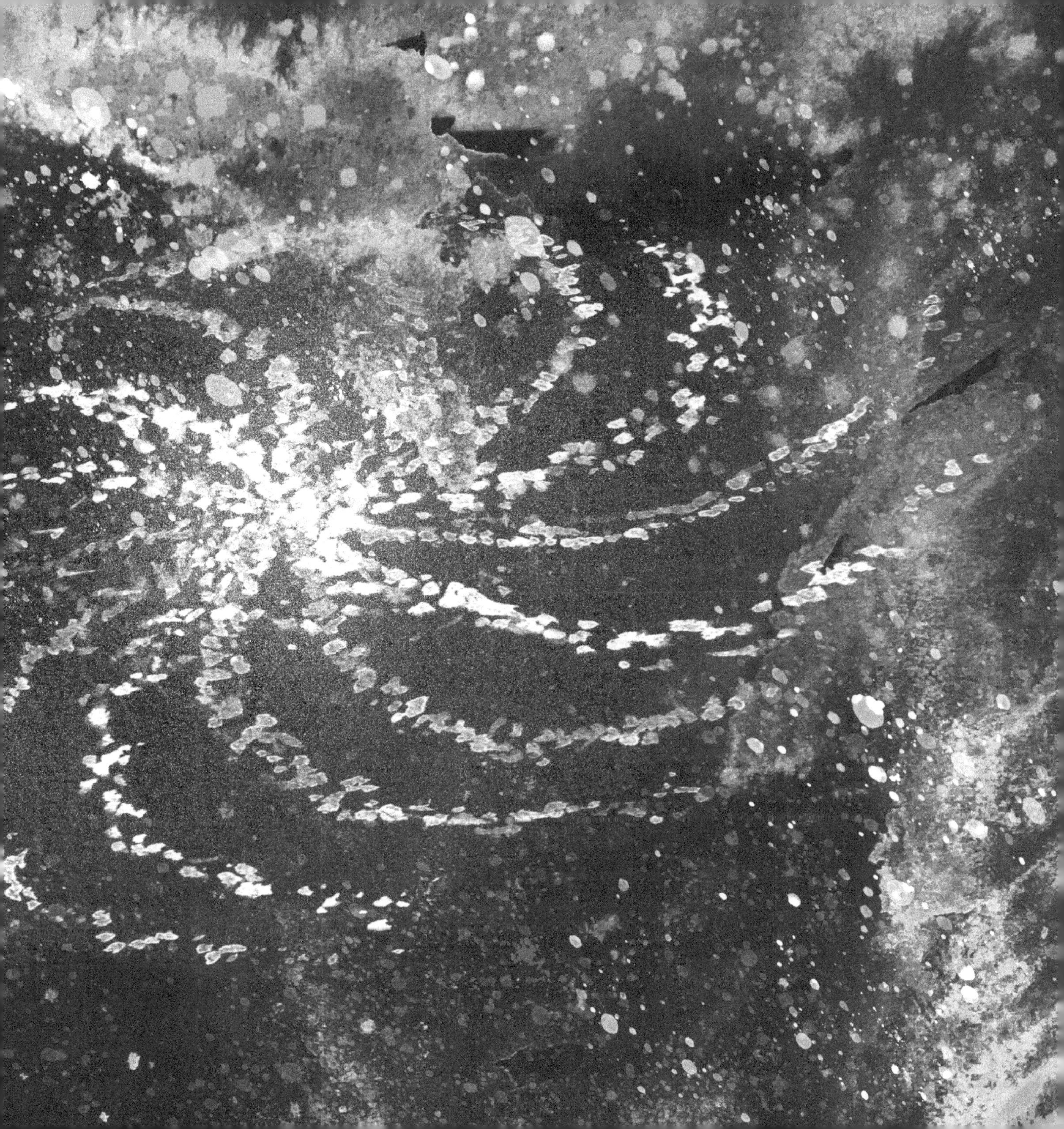

Our brain determines what's important through repetition or impression.

The term "sticky impressions" aptly describes the result of emotion, sensory input, and meaning coming together to create strong and lasting impressions that seem permanently glued in the brain.

For example, if you once nearly fell off a cliff, you might have a visceral reaction every time you approach the edge of a high place. When the amygdala is activated, the fear experienced leaves a powerful impression on us—because once, our survival may have depended on it.

A similar process is at work when we are learning a language. Having contextual meaning when we try to learn a new word or phrase helps us to remember because our brain relates it to what we already know. This is the reason watching TV and movies in another language is so beneficial to acquiring language: we see the real-world context and relate the meaning to our current understanding of that situation. Okay, maybe *Star Wars* isn't "real-world," but you get the point, young Jedi.

> **USE YOUR DICTIONARY!**
> *When reading, look up any words you don't understand. By gliding by misunderstood words and relying solely on context, we set ourself up for a "confusion trance." During this time, our attention to whatever we read next is muddled, creating a gap in our comprehension.*

Just as a web browser is our interface with the internet, allowing us to interact with all the information in the world, learning serves as the interface between the conscious and subconscious mind. We take information obtained through conscious attention and store it in the subconscious mind for later replay or retrieval. The conscious mind isn't always running the show, however. Subliminal learning, like listening to affirmations at a low volume while sleeping, is an example of subconscious learning, as we aren't actively aware of what we're hearing. Similarly, a child picking up a language over time through exposure, and without conscious effort, illustrates how the subconscious mind absorbs information passively.

We learn by association, observation, practice, and conditioning, and we remember through repetition and impression. Our learning really shows up in our doing.

Doing is learning in action: if we don't do what we've learned, how can we say we've truly learned it?

> *"We remember what moves us—learning sticks when the heart is stirred."*
>
> **April Norris**

New experiences aid learning and memory. Your brain has the innate ability
to physically change itself when faced with new, challenging experiences.
This ability is called neuroplasticity. Neural networks are just gangs of neurons
that form connected pathways. These pathways are created and reshaped when
we process new information and experiences. They are then reinforced through
repetition. Hebb's law states that neurons that repeatedly fire together wire
together more strongly.[33]

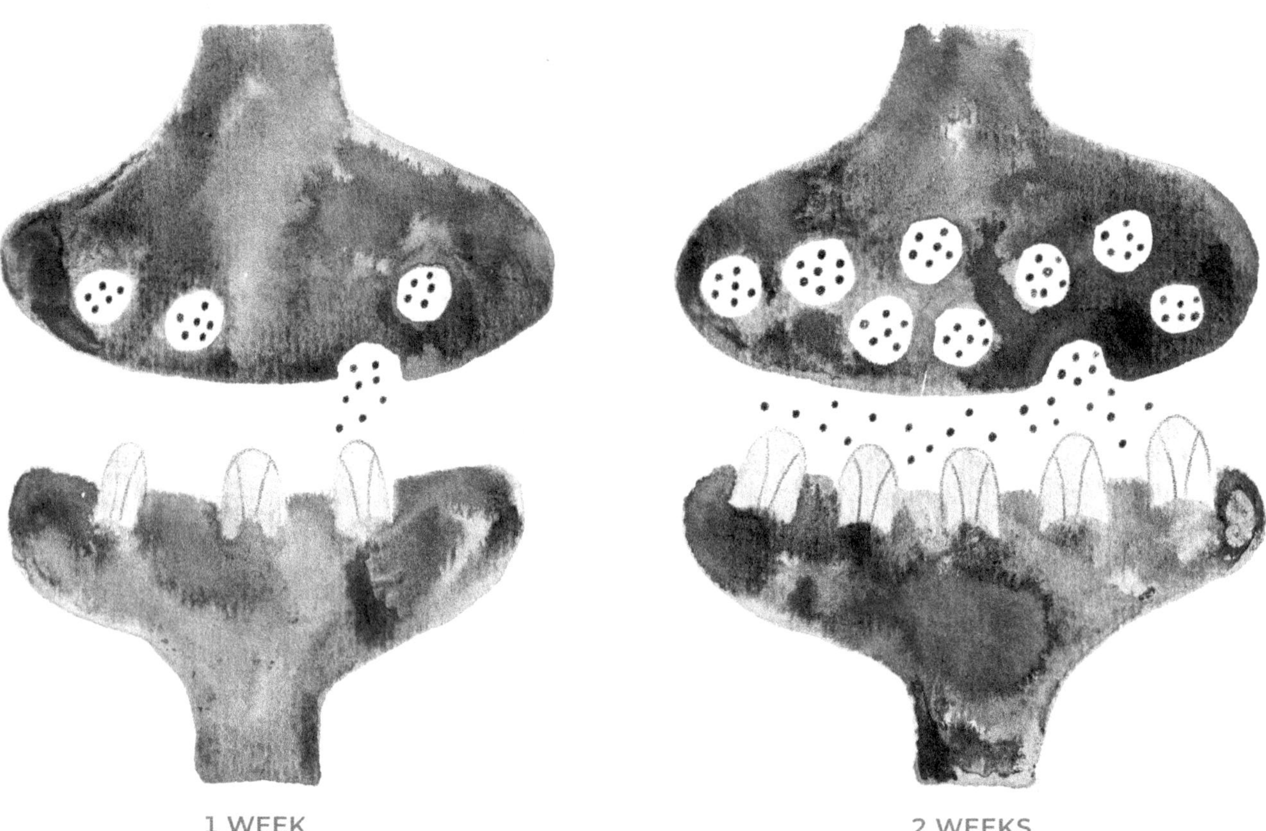

We now know the brain stays moldable for life. Neuroplasticity means you can literally reshape your brain by changing your mind—rearranging the pathways your neurons travel as your thoughts learn new choreography. Yes, you can teach an old dog new tricks. The mind can grasp a concept from just a few examples and stretch that insight across entirely new situations. It's a shape-shifting marvel, a living cathedral of circuits that rewrite themselves as you grow.

Even our brightest machines still stumble here. Humans: 1. Robots: still loading...

Humans carry what code can't quite capture—flexible, self-directed understanding; knowledge rooted in sensory experience; and learning infused with emotion, nuance, and meaning.

And yet, being human doesn't make transformation effortless. Unlike robots, **breaking habitual thought patterns is challenging because we are biologically driven to maintain homeostasis.** Our nervous systems prefer efficiency, often defaulting to familiar neural pathways simply because they require less energy.

That's why leaving our comfort zone can feel uncomfortable—or even scary—without a growth mindset and regular practice. When old neural pathways fire automatically, change can feel like an uphill battle.

Fortunately, the brain is designed to keep learning and evolving. It remains adaptable throughout life and can always be upgraded through conscious awareness and practice. By intentionally rearranging how we use existing neural circuits, we can break habitual patterns of thinking and rewire the brain's pathways for growth and transformation.

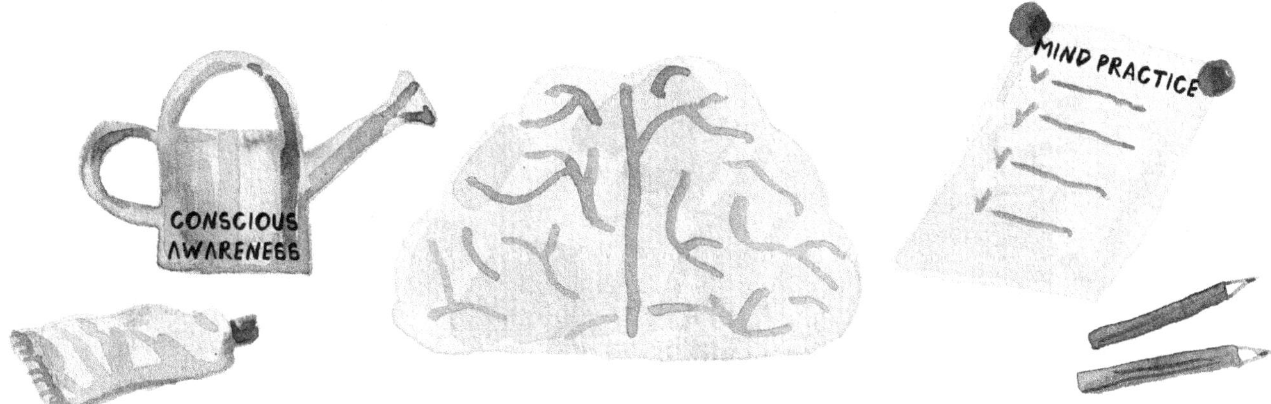

Working Memory

Working memory, the partner of attention, provides a temporary mental workspace that allows us to hold and manipulate information while referring to other details. It enables key cognitive functions such as comprehension, planning, reasoning, and problem-solving.

Uncertainty remains about its exact limits, including how much information it can retain and how quickly it decays, but, without active rehearsal, information in working memory typically has a lifespan of 10 to 15 seconds—sometimes even less.

Working memory is on the job during tasks like solving math problems in our head or when we follow a recipe and remember not to add the same ingredient twice.

Working memory is also at play when we read or listen to audiobooks. As we see or hear words, it temporarily holds them in place until the entire sentence is processed, allowing us to grasp the overall meaning and context.

Take this sentence, for example:

"Most people agree that when the weather is clear, the temperature is not too hot, and your body is in good health, it is an ideal time to go for a hike."

Holding the unifying information until the end of the sentence is quite taxing on our working memory.

The sentence is much easier to comprehend when the main point is introduced first:

"Most people agree that the ideal time to go for a hike is when the weather is clear, the temperature is not too hot, and your body is in good health."

Therefore, you could say that working memory also contributes to good writing! We can think of our working memory as the lobby of our mind. Information enters, checks in with reception, and gets processed according to its relevance. If that information has a VIP emotional pass, it gets sent to the long-term memory suite.

If that info is the name of someone you just met?
Bye, Felicia...or was it Felicity?

Willpower

Simply put, willpower is the ability to control our impulses and actions. It empowers us to resist short-term gratification in favor of obtaining our long-term goals.

Will has many names: resolve, self-control, determination, and self-discipline—to name a few.

You can think of willpower as a cognitive override—using the conscious mind to tame the emotional or habitual impulses of the subconscious mind.

Willpower is saying no to that chocolate cookie that caught your eye while ordering your coffee. The rich, fudgy one with chocolate chips glistening and exuding a intoxicating aroma that seduces your olfactory senses—"Must be fresh!"—Yeah, that one.

"Treat yourself!" the barista sings from behind the counter when she catches you staring at this gastronomical vision. You feel a bead of sweat forming at your temple. The urge is intense.

Then, seemingly out of nowhere, an empowering image of your healthy future self pops into your mind's eye. "I already had breakfast, and I'm trying to cut back on sugar," you reason to yourself.

"Just the coffee, thanks," you reply virtuously. Phew! Close call.

Willpower is an emotionally driven state in which we focus on a desired future outcome rather than immediate gratification. When our self-control fails, it's because an emotionally charged stimulus overrode our rational mind, leading to impulsive actions. Our actions greatly depend on whether our focus is in the future or the present.

Ironically, short-term gratification makes us feel on top of the world in the moment, but that pleasure is short-lived—and often leads to an eventual crash. When we make choices that are aligned with our goals and put in the hard work, we feel better about ourselves and empowered to continue on our path to self-actualization.

We can think of willpower as a muscle that can be strengthened through regular exertion of self-control—but can also become fatigued from overuse.

Some research suggests that willpower depletion has a physical basis in the brain.[34] People whose willpower is depleted show decreased activity in a brain region associated with cognition—the anterior cingulate cortex. Other studies have shown that low blood glucose levels result in an impaired ability to exhibit self-control.[35] This suggests that the brain consumes glucose faster than can be replenished when under the heavy workload of trying to say no to that cookie. You just need to eat the cookie to restore the required glucose, right?

Willpower depletion affects our self-control in all spheres, and has an impact on behaviors such as food consumption and substance use. This is why having a long list of New Year's resolutions is a terrible idea.

It is much more effective to focus your efforts on one goal at a time.

The good news is that positive moods and beliefs can strengthen our resilience to depletion. Having strong sense of internal motivation buffers us from the early effects of willpower depletion.

WILLPOWER IS LIKE A MUSCLE: IT CAN BE STRENGTHENED

Know your why. Imagine a future in which you've achieved your goal. Understanding your deeper motivation (your why) removes ambiguity and gives you a clear reason to guide your decisions.

Hold yourself accountable. Track your actions and notice if they align with your goal. Regularly ask yourself: "Am I consistently making choices that bring me closer to my goal, or are they leading me away from it?" This could involve journaling, keeping notes on your phone, or using a calendar to monitor your progress.

Remember that disciplined choices lead to greater fulfillment in the long-term. While instant gratification might feel good in the moment, the sense of pride and accomplishment that comes from staying aligned with your goals is far more rewarding.

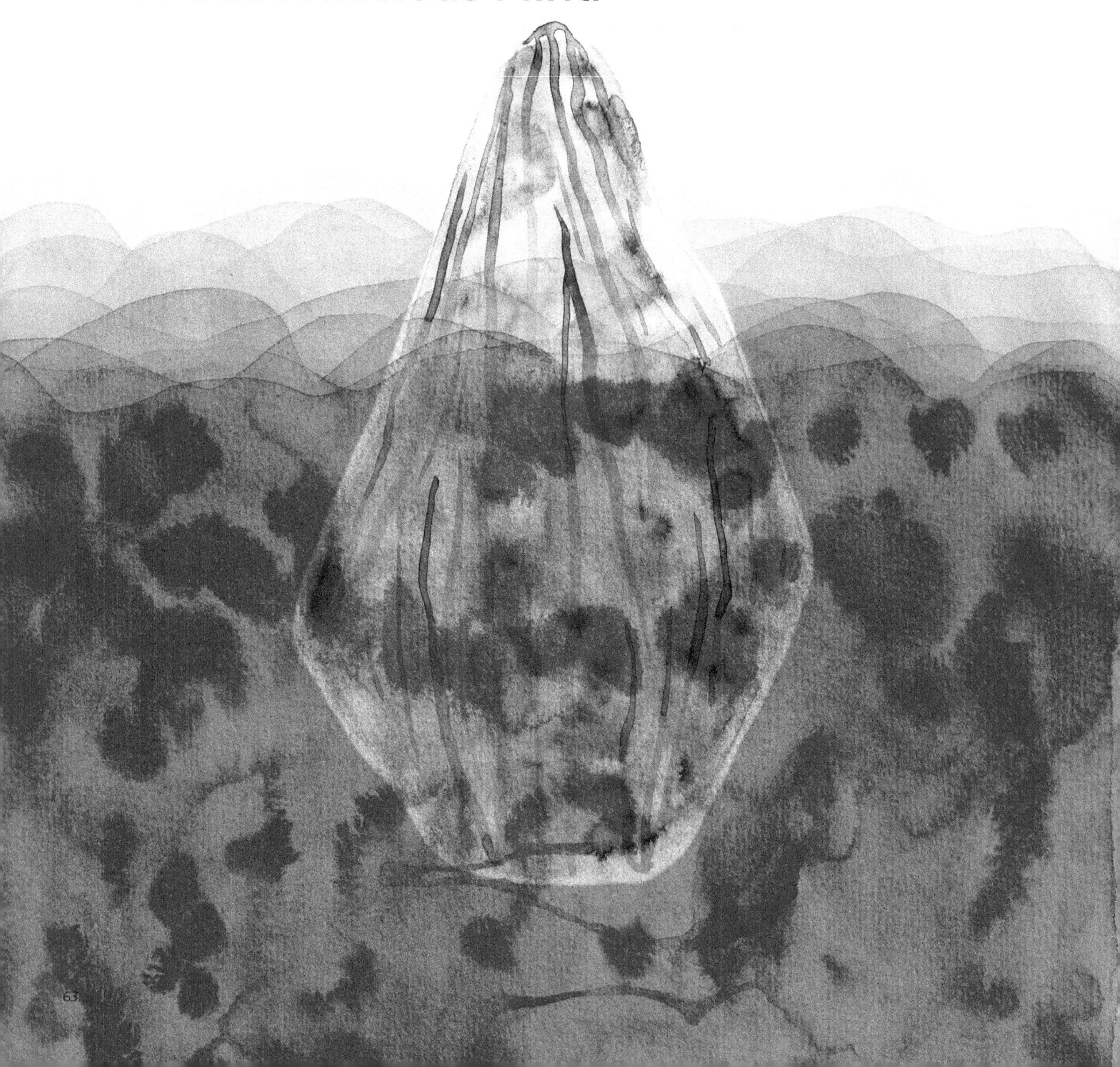

The Subconscious Mind

THE SUBCONSCIOUS MIND IS HOME TO OUR:

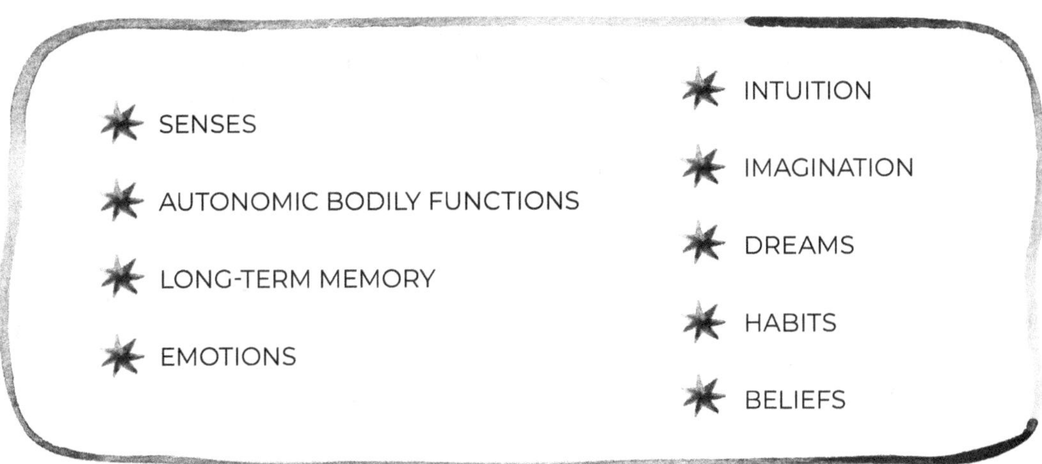

If your conscious mind were a tricycle, your subconscious mind would be a rocket ship.

A whole lot of things go on in the subconscious mind, from bodily functions and pattern recognition to dreaming and intuition. And much of it is happening simultaneously. According to neuro-linguistic programming experts, the subconscious mind processes an estimated four hundred billion (400,000,000,000) bits of information per second.

The conscious mind? Only around 2,000 bits.

You may remember how sluggish dial-up internet speeds were back in the 90s—around 56,000 bits per second[36]—like a single-lane road clogged with slow-moving traffic, painfully slow and prone to halts.

When life get busy or overwhelming, our minds don't usually freeze like those old modems did when a phone call cut the line. Instead, we keep moving forward and navigating around obstacles, much like traffic flowing along a multi-lane highway.

CONSCIOUS

SUBCONSCIOUS

Most people take about 20,000 breaths a day, and our hearts beat 100,000 times a day, both without any conscious effort on our part. The subconscious mind is busy operating these involuntary systems.

The subconscious mind doesn't analyze, make comparisons or reason. It obeys commands and follows programs. **It feels and automates.** It uses a language of emotion, story, metaphor, and symbols—a language few people ever learn. A poet or mystic might say the subconscious mind is our link to the timeless divine.

NOW LET'S TAKE A DEEPER LOOK AT THE FUNCTIONS OF THE SUBCONSCIOUS MIND...

The Senses

"Principles for the Development of a Complete Mind:
Study the science of art. Study the art of science.
Develop your senses—especially learn how to see.
Realize that everything connects to everything else."[38]

Leonardo da Vinci

"The world is full of magic things,
patiently waiting for our senses
to grow sharper."[39]

Eden Philpotts

Our senses bring us to the borders of our reality and can transport us into new realms.

At their most basic level, **the five senses**—sound, touch, sight, taste, and smell—**are all forms of touch.** With our eyes, we feel photons of light. The ears touch vibrations in the air.

Taste and smell are the results of molecules touching receptors in our mouth and nose. It is no coincidence that brain matter and skin come from the same type of dermis, and both contain the same type of neuropeptides. Our five sensory faculties are the key to passing signals through the brain and our entire nervous system.

Our senses, especially touch, link directly to the body's inner pharmacy. Sensory stimulation can spark biochemical releases of self-generated "medicine."

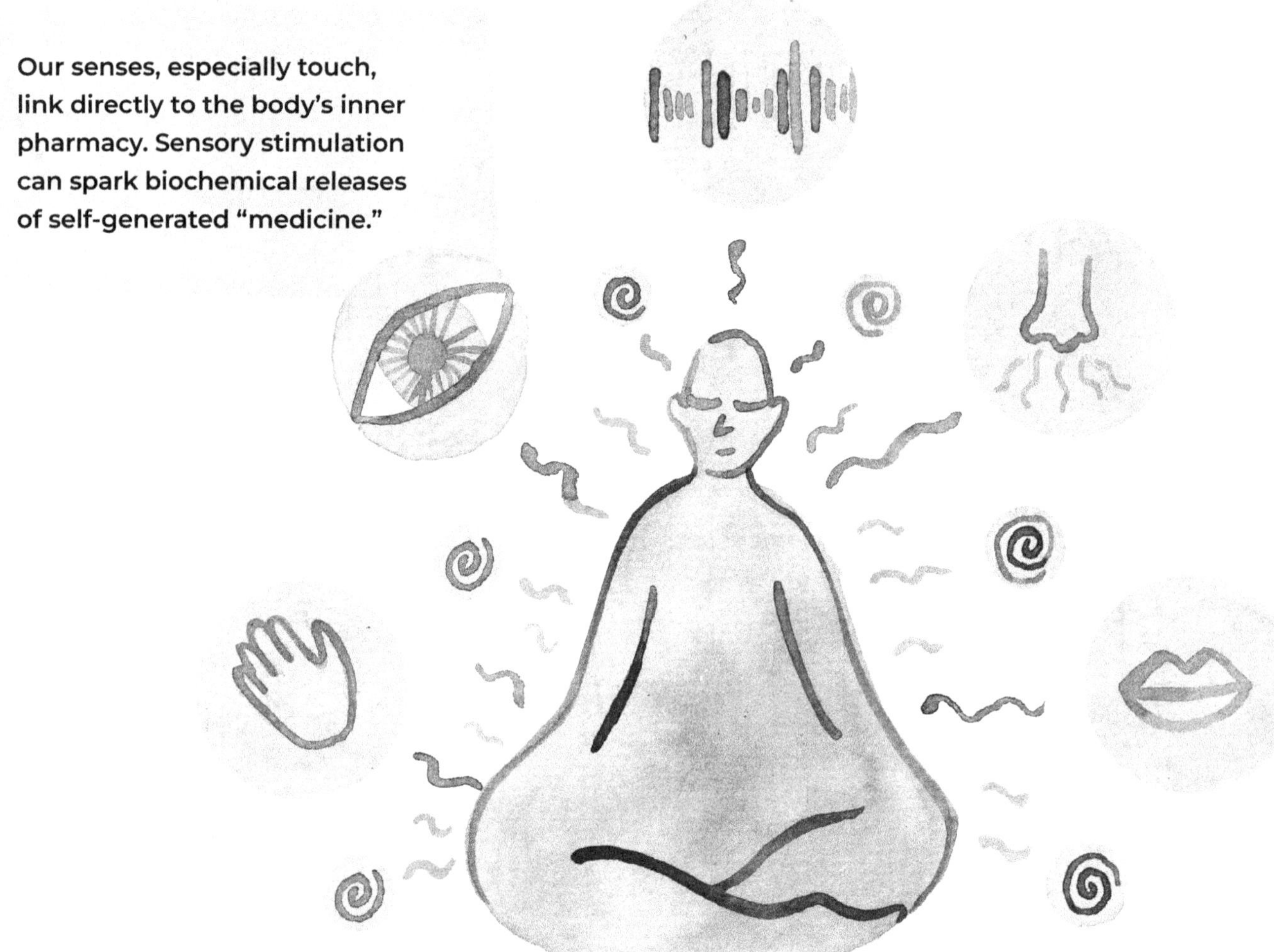

What we experience through our senses, we label as real. However, we can't detect the ultrasound waves that bats use to navigate their environments or the infrared light that snakes can perceive. Even though these frequencies are not part of our perceived reality, they are real and these animals therefore experience a reality that is very different from ours.

The word "senses" comes from the Latin sentīre, which means "to feel." Our senses provide a shortcut to triggering emotions directly, and at times intensely. The smell of fresh apple pie transports us to the joys of our childhood, the sight of an ex may flood our hearts with fear, and the pitter-patter of rain on the roof brings a soothing comfort. Our senses have a preverbal influence on our mood and physical body, communicating beyond language.

ANIMAL SUPER SENSES

Migratory birds: magneto reception

Elephants: seismic communication

Octopuses: touch-taste integration

Sharks: electroreception

Dolphins: echolocation

Cats: night vision

DID YOU KNOW...

A dog's sense of smell is thousands of times stronger than ours...dogs can even tell time with their sense of smell.[40]

The senses are simply different ways of interpreting data from the environment. The somatosensory cortex of the parietal lobes processes information from the peripheral nerves, which are communication pathways that connect to the spinal cord. **Sensory processing areas can be interchangeable;** for example, in blind individuals, the visual cortex is reassigned to process touch and sound instead.

The neuroplasticity of our brains is pretty wild. Researchers are even teaching blind people to "see" with their tongues! Even though the experience is not quite the same as vision through our eyes, the incoming data through the tongue can be interpreted as a visual experience in the mind.

SYNESTHESIA

A phenomenon of cross-sense association called **synesthesia** can also occur. This is when one sensory experience is immediately perceived with another sense, such as a certain sound occurring with a color or shape.[41]

Smell

The primordial centers for emotion evolved from the olfactory lobe, eventually encircling the top of the brainstem. As evolution continued, layers were added, forming rings that developed into the limbic system, which includes the memory-related amygdala and hippocampus.

Research suggests that smell triggers more emotional memories than sight or sound.[43] This is because the olfactory bulb is directly connected to the amygdala and hippocampus, while other senses, like sight and taste, first go through the brain's relay station, the thalamus.

As you remember from earlier, the amygdala is the emotional center, and the hippocampus is responsible for episodic memories, which is why memories associated with scent tend to be of a time and place and are formed from a first-person perspective.[44]

A quirky and fascinating fact: a tribe in New Guinea says goodbye by putting a hand in each other's armpit, withdrawing it, and stroking it over themselves. Try it with your friends!

According to research published in the journal *Science*, inside our nasal cavity, in an area smaller than a postage stamp, there are five to six million olfactory receptor cells that help us distinguish up to a trillion different smells. With such impressive ability, the nose is the last body part that we should be picking on. That one's for you Dad ;)

Anyone who's ever had a drink shoot out of their nose thanks to a perfectly timed joke knows firsthand just how connected the mouth and nose are. Through that connection, our sense of taste is intrinsically linked to our sense of smell. When we chew, molecules in the food take the back door to the nasal passage, giving us a perceived flavor.

This is why when you smell something delicious, you can almost taste it. It's also why people plug their noses when eating something they don't want to taste. You can test this by plugging your nose and eating something like chocolate; you will only taste sweetness without the rich, distinctive aroma of chocolate.

Scent is like a muscle—by bringing conscious awareness to it throughout your day, you can improve your sense of smell and **expand the boundaries of your reality.**

Taste

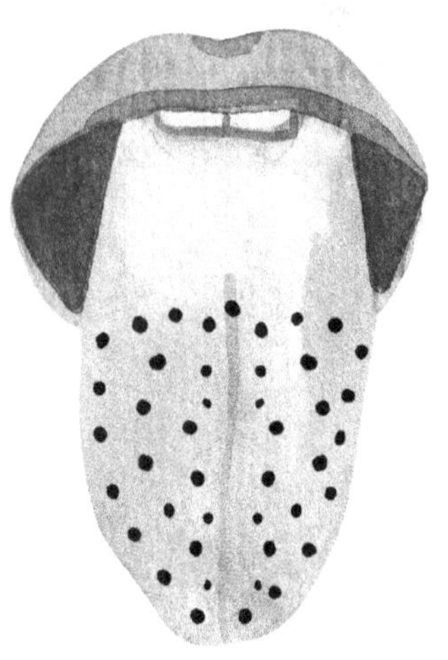

Adults have between 2,000 and 8,000 taste buds, each containing 50 to 100 taste receptor cells. These cells convey information to a neuron, which then relays it to the brain. Each taste bud is replaced every two weeks approximately, but they are replaced less often as we get older, resulting in a loss of taste acuity over time.

From a survival perspective, our sense of taste lets us know if something is safe or harmful to eat. Judging by the way milkshakes taste, one would think that they are the elixir of life!

Our five basic tastes are sweetness, sourness, saltiness, bitterness, and umami which means savoriness.

Conventional belief held that certain areas of the tongue were responsible for detecting specific tastes, but later research has disproven this notion.[45] Although certain areas like the sides and tip of the tongue are more sensitive to taste, all areas can discern each of the basic tastes.

The tongue can also perceive other sensations that are not typically considered basic tastes, such as pungency or spiciness, coolness, like in mints and menthol, and astringency, like in red wine, which creates a puckering sensation caused by tannins and calcium oxalate.

TASTE FACTS:

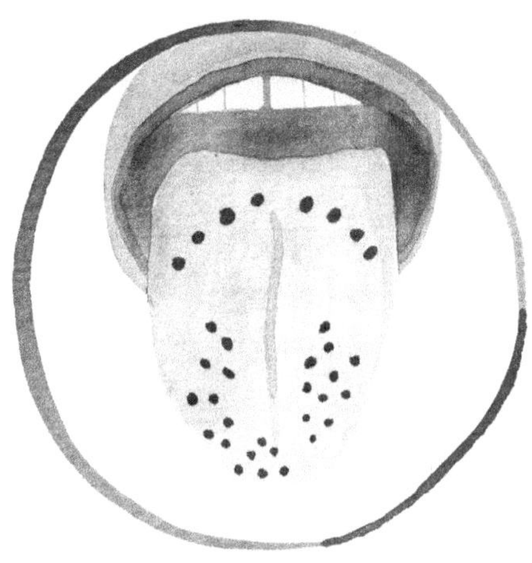

Everyone has a different number of taste buds.

Eating sweet foods helps form a memory of a meal.

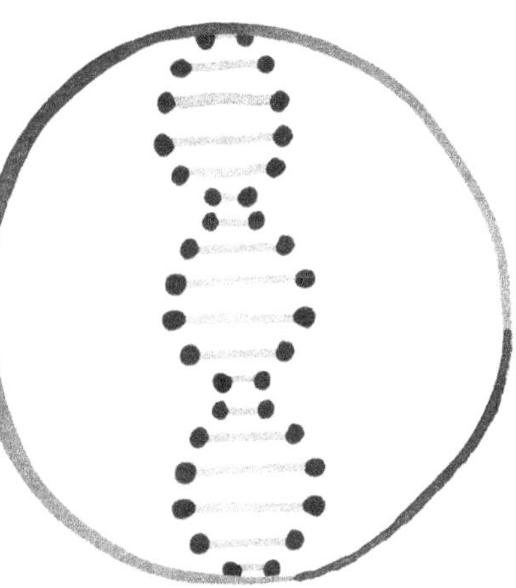

Your genes influence whether you think cilantro tastes like soap.

Touch

Let's touch on a somewhat touchy subject now: touch!

This silly sentence shows that our language is steeped in phrases and metaphors related to the sense of touch. For example, you might get in touch with an employer, lose touch with a dear friend, or keep in touch with your parents.

Maybe you touch up your essay to add more of a personal touch. Just a touch, though; it already looks great!

Okay, we're not going to do the same with "feel"—you feel me?

We put a lot of importance on touch because it's a vital and primal part of how we communicate and bond.

When we are born, our visual systems are still very immature, and touch is one of the first ways we interact with the world and communicate with our parents. Research suggests that touch is our most potent sense for communication.[46]

Skin-to-skin contact releases the bonding hormone oxytocin. This hormone causes babies to seek out and latch to their mother's breast—breastfeeding then floods the body with more oxytocin. At any stage in our life, the release of oxytocin through touch builds trust, reduces stress hormones, and makes us feel connected.

Touch also produces a rich source of growth hormones and is imperative for the healthy development of babies. Research in both humans and dogs has shown that physical contact with the parent stimulates growth.[47] Studies have shown that a lack of touch suppresses growth hormone levels in babies, and even injections of growth hormones fail to stimulate growth without touch.

Skin-to-skin contact restores growth by reducing stress hormones and enabling growth hormone activity.

Our skin, which enables our sense of touch, is the body's largest organ and can weigh from six to ten pounds. It is alive and teeming with microorganisms. It protects us against germs, removes toxins, and regulates body temperature. It also has the unique ability to repair itself.

This capacity for self-repair is reliant on the immune system. The skin has many immune cells that defend the body against pathogens and play a critical role in preventing infection as well as healing tissue in the event of injury.

Here are some interesting anecdotes about the power of touch:

* A study at Purdue University Library showed that when a librarian casually touched one group of students and not the other, the touched group reported more satisfaction with the library and life in general.[48]

* In another study, participants temporarily held a coffee cup containing either warm or iced coffee while an employee filled out some basic forms. After arriving upstairs, participants were asked to rate a fictional person. Those who held the warm cup tended to rate the target person as "warmer"—more humane, trustworthy, and friendly—than those who had held the iced coffee.[49]

* Receiving a pat on the back from a teacher instilled kids with confidence, causing them to be twice as likely to speak up in class.[50]

* Patients who receive eye contact and touch from their doctor have lower mortality rates in complex diseases.[51]

Hearing

What we hear has a significant impact on our emotions. The sound of children laughing can bring a smile to our faces, our favorite song makes us want to sing and dance, and hearing a sudden crash can freeze us in our tracks, activating our primal survival systems.

Sound results from patterns of energy moving through the air that your brain interprets and assigns meaning to.

What we call sound is really a cascade of air molecules caused by the movement of an object. The lightning-fast snapping of a cricket's wings cracks like tiny thunderclaps causing waves that travel far into the night, while the slow and soft movement of our vocal cords produces whispers that only reach the intended recipient's ear.

Waves of sound roll like tides to our ears, making the eardrum vibrate. This, in turn, moves three tiny bones—which are the smallest bones of all 206 in the body. These bones press fluid in the inner ear against membranes that brush against tiny hairs. This movement triggers nearby nerve cells that telegraph messages to the brain, enabling us to hear.

The three tiny bones of the ear:

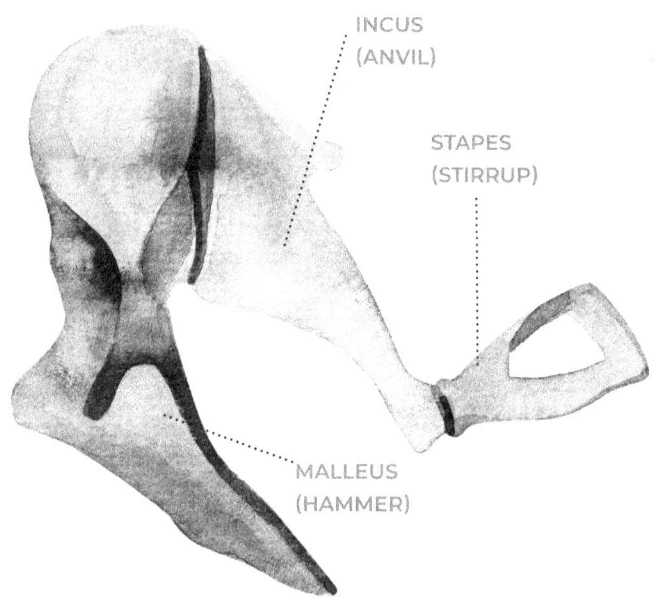

Sound travels through the air significantly slower (1,125 ft/s) than the speed of light (186,282 mi/s), which is why we often see a flash of lightning during a thunderstorm and hear the thunder a few moments later.

Noise pollution—the unwanted noise in our environment—can adversely affect our health.

Since our auditory system is fundamentally designed to keep us alive, constant noise keeps the amygdala on high alert, which can put us in a fight-or-flight response mode, making us feel stressed and anxious. In addition, a noisy environment can impair our ability to focus and disrupt our sleep quality, leading to further negative mental and physical symptoms. You can close your eyes but, unfortunately, you cannot close your ears. Earplugs anyone?

Sound can be used to lift objects through "acoustical levitation."[52]

Sight

I spy with my little eye...ten million pieces of sensory information per second!

Most of us consider our sight to be our most important sense. Probably because vision provides us with the most information about the world. For example, we can tell when strawberries look pale and sour versus deep red and ripe, recognize whether someone's facial expression is friendly or threatening, and detect when the light begins to dim in the sky, signaling that it's time to seek shelter.

The retina contains millions of receptors that perform countless calculations per second, making our eyes more sensitive than any camera.

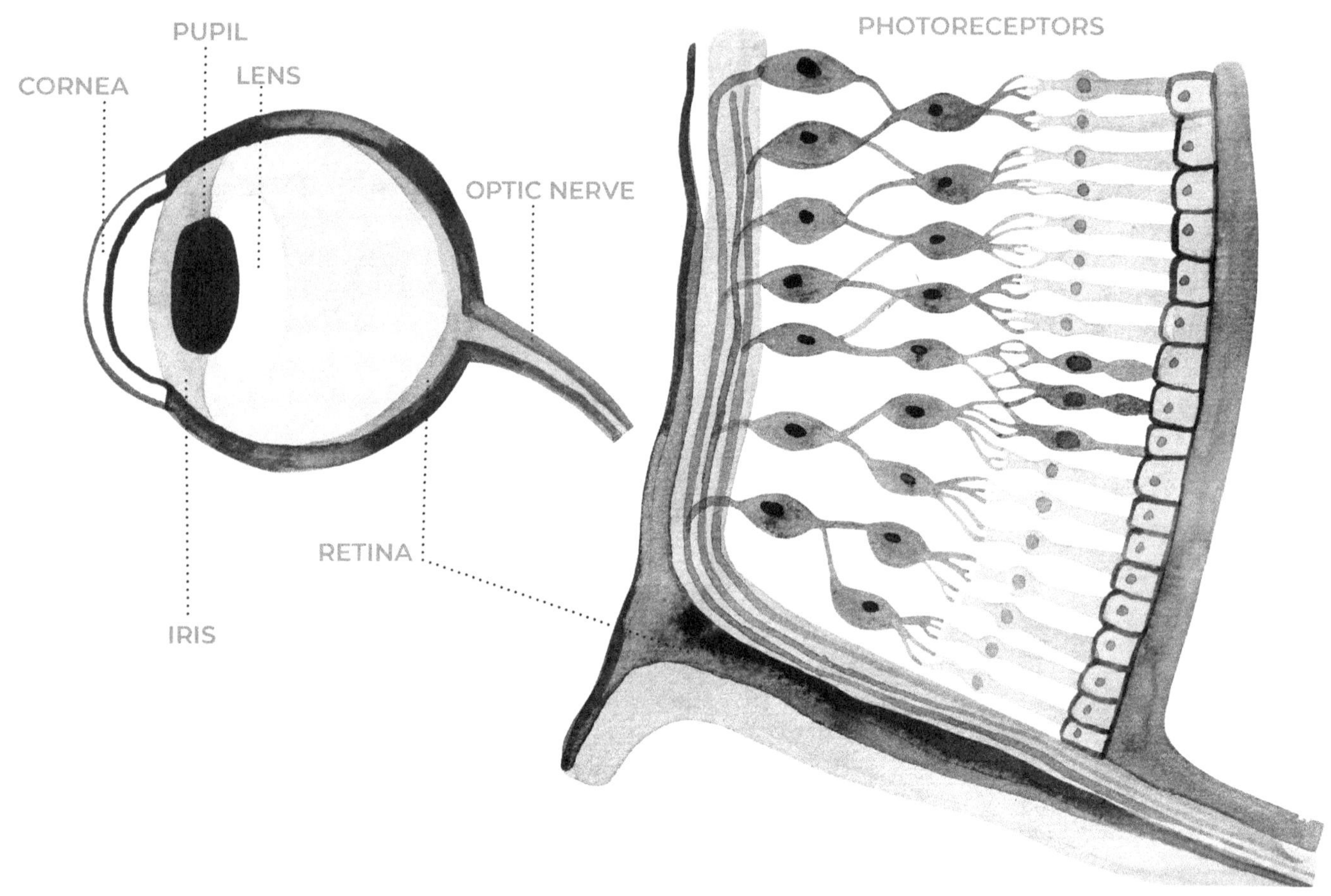

Color doesn't exist without light, and it occurs not in the world but in the mind. This is why you can barely see colors at night—everything appears desaturated without sufficient light.

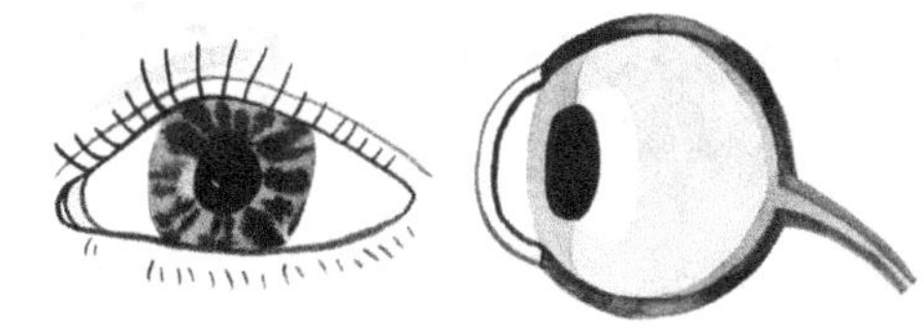

Isaac Newton's pioneering experiments with prisms revealed that white light is composed of a spectrum of colors, laying the foundation for modern color theory. By demonstrating that each color corresponds to light waves of different wavelengths, Newton provided a scientific basis that allowed artists to develop more sophisticated approaches, enhancing the emotional and psychological impact of their work. His insights into light and color also have significant implications for how we understand their effects on the human mind. The interplay of light and color can influence mood, perception, and cognitive function, making it a powerful tool in shaping human experience. Leveraging the principles of color theory established by Newton, we can create environments and artworks that evoke tailored mental and emotional responses that benefit mental well-being.

WAVELENGTHS OF LIGHT

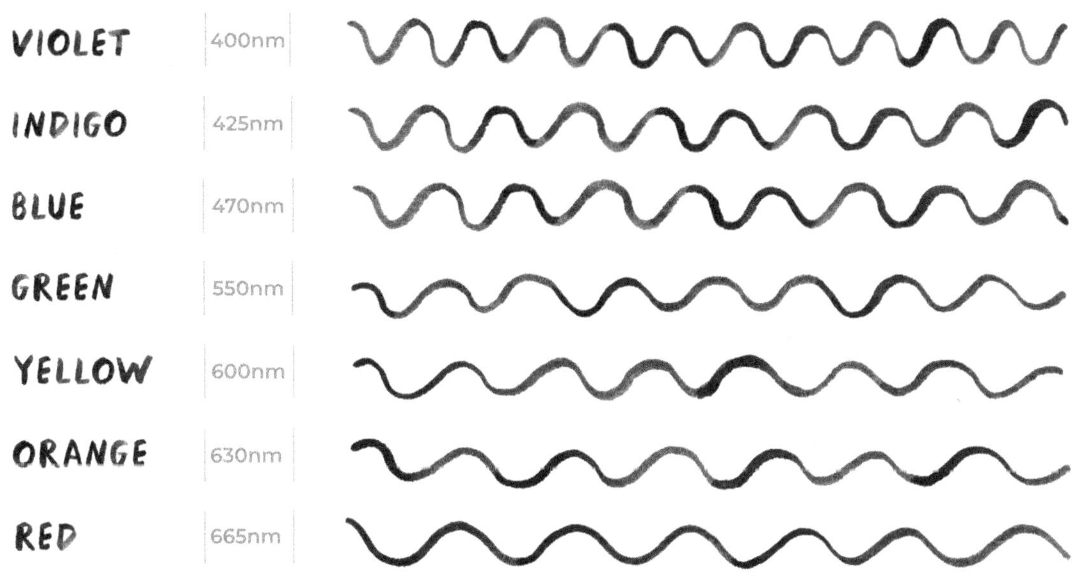

Our perception of color results from different wavelengths of light being reflected into our eyes. White light, such as from the sun, contains the full spectrum of wavelengths along with their corresponding colors. When we see an object that we perceive as white, it is because that object reflects all those wavelengths back to us, while conversely, black objects absorb all the wavelengths. A red rose would reflect the red wavelengths, a pine tree the green, and so on.

Autonomic Bodily Functions

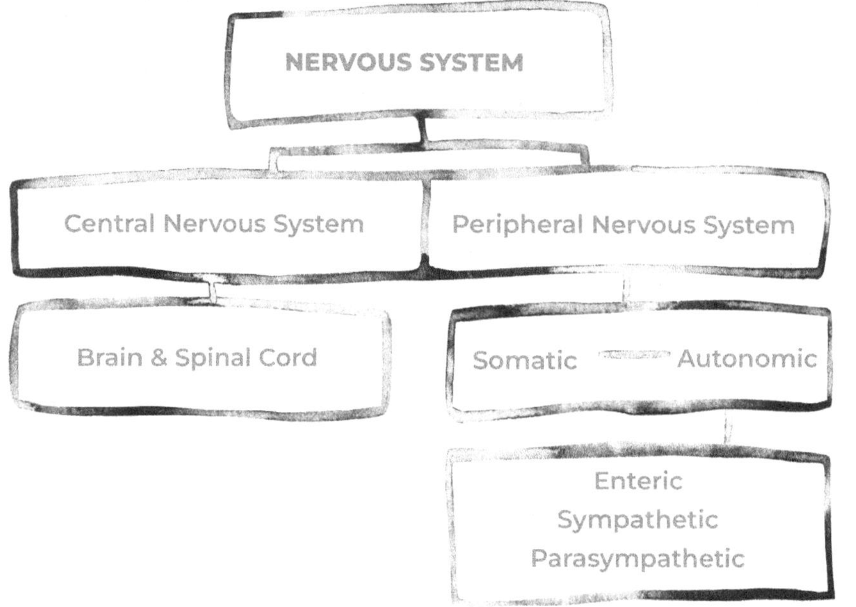

The subconscious mind plays a role in all the behind-the-scenes functions of your body that you don't consciously notice. It guides the autonomic nervous system to control organ function, and regulate body temperature, digestion, breathing, and heart rate—to name a few.

You can think of autonomic as automatic—operating involuntarily, outside of your conscious awareness.

The **sympathetic** division of the autonomic nervous system governs alertness. It revs up our bodies to prepare us for survival-based action, speeding up our heart rate, and dilating our pupils. As mentioned at the beginning of the book, it is responsible for our fight-or-flight response.

The **parasympathetic** division serves as a calming counterbalance to the sympathetic subsystem. It helps bring the body back to baseline, redirecting energy toward digestion, repair, and pro-social behaviors that support connection and bonding. This relaxed state is commonly known as the rest-and-digest response.

These yin and yang systems are primal, designed millions of years ago to keep us safe in a world full of predators and storms. But today, the landscape has changed dramatically. While we're relatively safe from those ancient threats, we now face a host of modern stressors in a society where dysfunction has become the norm.

A few examples include:

* The need to be accepted by our peers is an ancient drive for a social species like ours, however, we now face social comparisons and judgments amplified by the introduction of connecting technologies such as the internet and social media.

* Our economic structures pressure us to work tiringly long hours just to make a living. Depending on our socioeconomic status and location in the world, financial stability can be a considerable burden on our nervous system.

* Urbanization has disconnected us from nature and, ultimately, from each other. Cities can overwhelm our systems with constant noise and stimulation. And the close proximity to so many strangers can subtly encourage us to withdraw, ignore, or even distrust our fellow humans.

* Societal expectations about who we should be, how we should act, and what we should strive for to be "successful" also increase our stress load.

The ability of the body to balance the sympathetic and parasympathetic states is crucial for our overall wellness. This process of self-regulation is known as homeostasis and refers to our body's ability to maintain stability in response to changing external conditions. Trauma can dysregulate our nervous systems, making it difficult to digest our experiences and emotions.

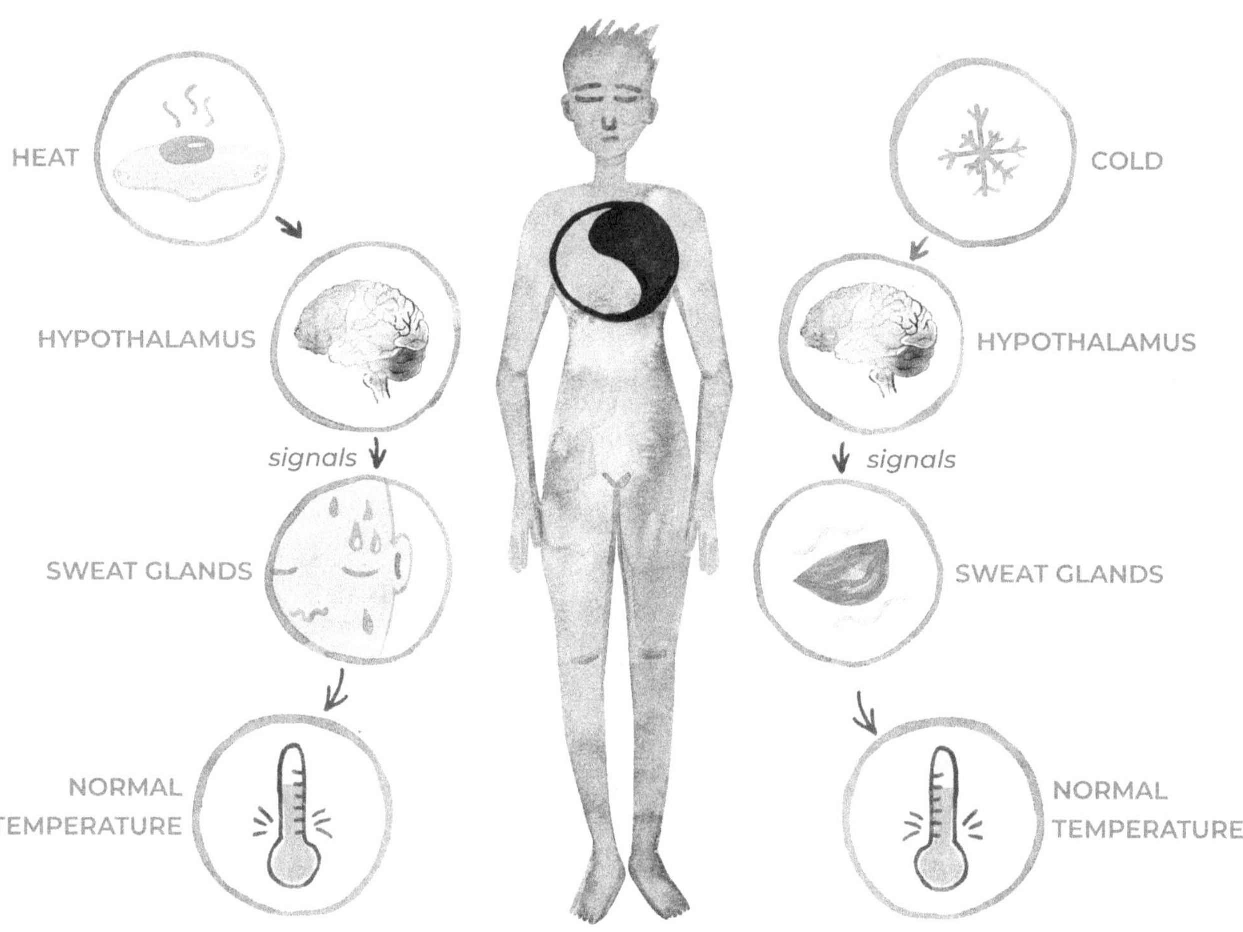

There is mounting evidence supporting body-based approaches that help regulate the nervous system and promote healing from trauma. Examples include mindfulness, yoga, meditation, and slow, deep breathing.

Even if we're not experiencing nervous system dysregulation, these practices can be invaluable during times of stress, helping to calm the body and anchor us in the present moment.

The final division of the autonomic nervous system, the enteric nervous system, is often called our brain–gut connection or second brain. Composed of two thin layers containing more than 100 million nerve cells, it lines the entire gastrointestinal tract and manages a wide range of functions—from swallowing and releasing digestive enzymes to eliminating waste.

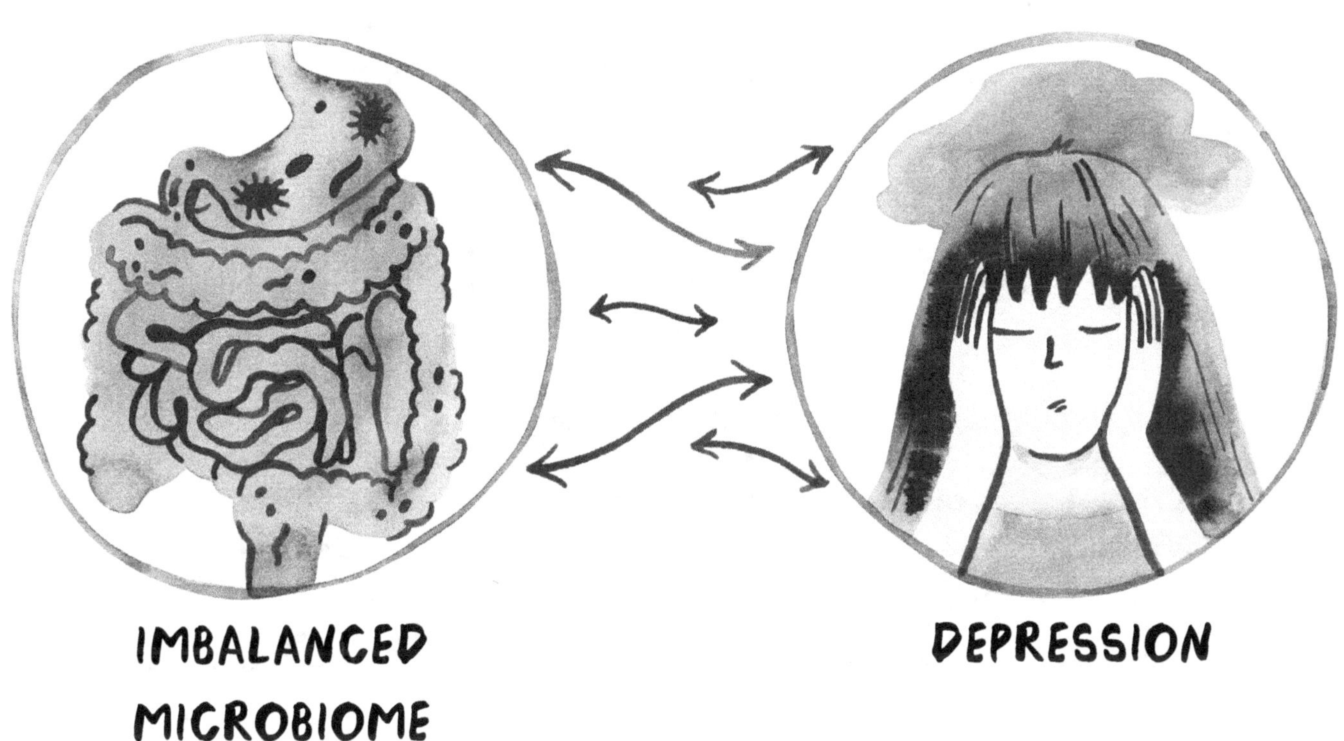

Researchers have found evidence that gastrointestinal irritation, such as irritable bowel syndrome (IBS), constipation, or diarrhea, may send signals to the central nervous system that trigger mood swings.[53] Functional bowel problems may even be linked to the development of anxiety and depression.

Long Term Memory

Odin's ravens, Huginn (Thought) and Munin (Memory), soar across Midgard each day, gathering knowledge from every corner of the world. Upon their return, they whisper their discoveries to Odin. The ravens are living symbols of his vast intelligence and the vital roles of thought and memory in understanding life's mysteries. Their flight reflects the Viking belief in the profound connection between consciousness, perception, and wisdom—reminding us that reflection and knowledge shape how we see the world.

Life is a tapestry woven from the threads of our memories.

If you believe in the idea of reincarnation, you might say that memories are the only thing we take with us when we die.

We carry our experiences with us through our lives like stars in the universe of our mind, some burning bright and others slowly fading in luminosity over the eons. Memories unite us with the ones we love.

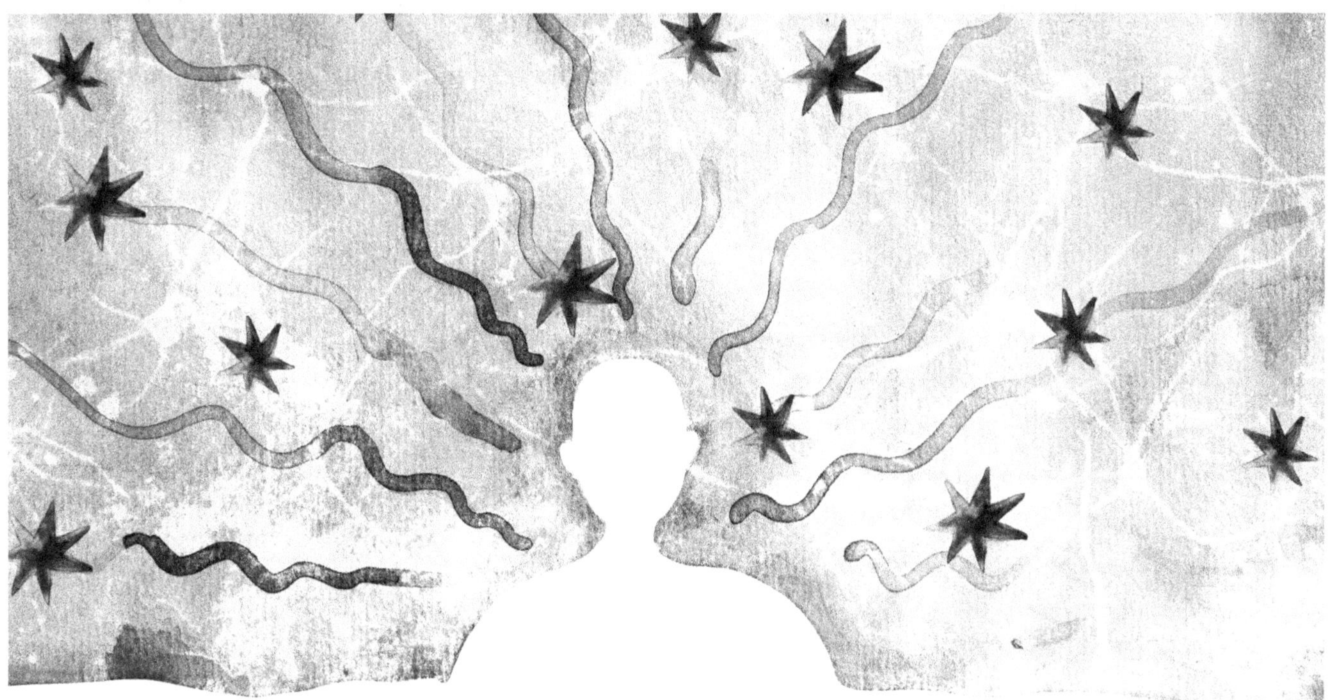

So how does memory work?

There are generally two types of memory: implicit and explicit. Implicit memories are formed without conscious effort and include skills or habits, such as riding a bike, driving, or brushing your teeth. These memories often feel automatic and are rooted in repetition. In contrast, explicit memories require intentional effort to store and recall, like remembering someone's name, the time of an appointment, or facts from a history lesson. Together, these memory types form the foundation of how we navigate and understand the world, balancing unconscious routines with conscious learning.

MEMORY CONNECTIONS

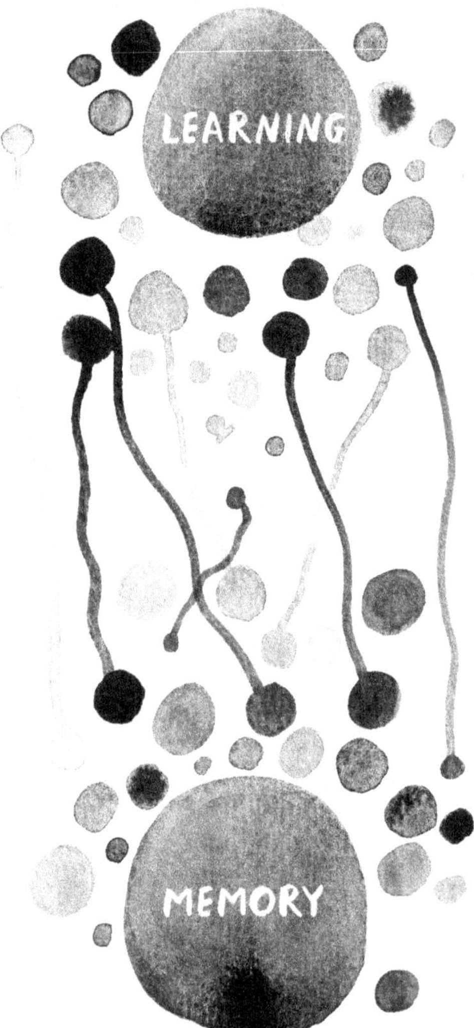

If learning is all about making new synaptic connections, remembering is all about keeping them connected.

Memory is both abstract and concrete. Abstract, because ideas and images seem to appear on an imaginary screen in your mind's eye; concrete, because memories physically strengthen neural connections, creating a tangible network of stored information.

These networks are vast. A single neuron can participate in multiple memories, linking to different networks depending on the information. When new information becomes a memory, fresh connections form. Much like binary code in computers, neurons either fire or don't, creating unique patterns that encode memories.

Implicit memories are effortless. Once we learn to drive a car or ride a bike, it becomes second nature—we don't think about every step; we just do it. The brain fires clusters of neurons, enabling us to act without conscious thought or deliberate recall.

Conditioned beliefs are essentially implicit memories— patterns of thinking and being shaped by repetition until they become habits. These memories influence how we experience and respond to the world, priming us to expect love from certain people or to shut down in conflict.

Our habits and "auto-pilot" moments are everyday examples of implicit memory at work.

We create implicit memories in two primary ways: first, through repetition and second, as a response to highly emotional personal experiences. Our favorite moments in life are richly sensual and richly emotional. When we associate a memory with a strong emotion, we create a longer-term memory than if we simply learned a fact and stored it semantically.

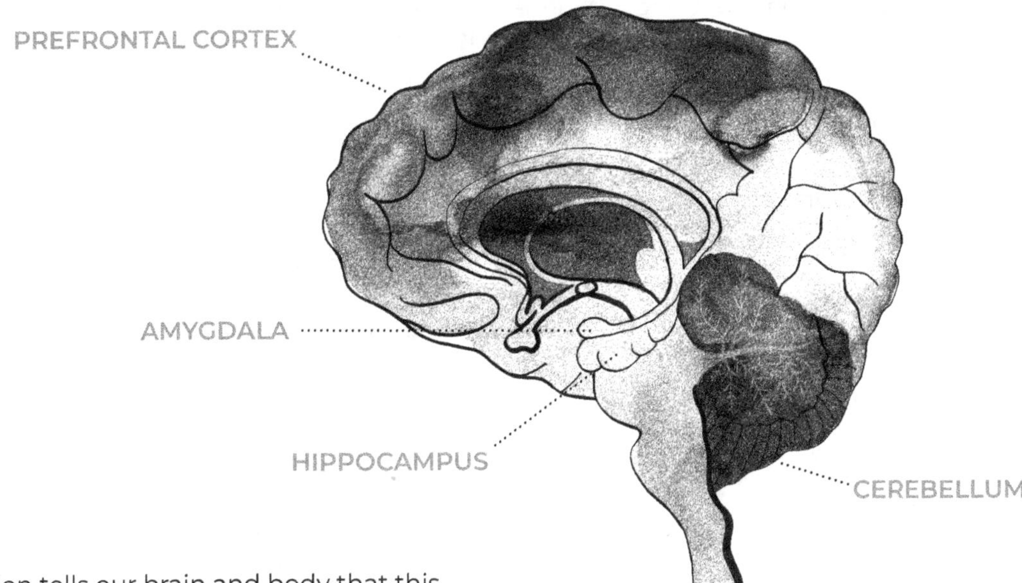

Emotion tells our brain and body that this information is important and must be stored. The experience gets branded in our minds. This process evolved to aid us in survival; you will definitely remember where that den was after being chased by a massive bear.

As you may recall from earlier in the book (come on, hippocampus!), the brain areas associated with memory are:

- ✸ **Prefrontal cortex:** language and logic memory
- ✸ **Amygdala:** fear-based memory
- ✸ **Hippocampus:** episodic memory, conscious recollection, recognition
- ✸ **Cerebellum:** procedural memory, motor skills

Look out! Amygdala has entered the chat!

The **amygdala** is like the brain's alarm system. It is always on the lookout for threats and can quickly and automatically trigger the fight-or-flight response when it perceives one. It does most of the brain's emotional processing, acting as a storehouse for emotional memory and generating responses related to fear and pleasure. Without the amygdala, life is stripped of personal meaning and passion.

However, due to the speed and automatic nature of threat detection, an overactive amygdala can cause our bodies to activate a stress response before our prefrontal cortex has time to rationalize the threat. For example, based on a previous memory of a bad experience, we might activate a full-blown stress response before a job interview when we're not actually in any danger. *"What's my greatest strength? Well, my amygdala is very energetic."*

When we are in the midst of a new experience, all our senses become engaged in the event. Joe Dispenza contends that if knowledge feeds the mind through the brain, experience feeds the mind through the body. What we see, smell, hear, taste, touch, and feel sends a synchronous crescendo of sensory stimuli through the five different pathways to the brain all at once. When that data reaches the brain, "jungles of neurons" fire and reorganize. An enormous release of chemical neurotransmitters occurs and new synaptic patterns begin to form, mapping that experience as new memories in the form of neural networks. The release of different brain chemicals produces specific feelings. Consequently, **the end product of every experience is a feeling or emotion.**[54]

Feelings are chemical memories—we remember experiences better because we remember how they felt.

When it comes to forming explicit (intentional) memories, we first store data in our working memory. Unfortunately, our working memory is a fickle beast to deal with. We can only hold between four and seven pieces of information for around 15 seconds, and our working memory is highly susceptible to distraction, discarding information when new information is presented.

However, we can hold information in our working memory longer through verbal repetition, also known as rehearsal.

Concentration, repetition, and emotion are the secret sauce for transferring information from your working memory to your long-term memory.

Concentration is key to forming neural connections, especially when we are processing purely semantic data. Without focused attention, no long-lasting synaptic connections can be made, and memories might not be stored. The second ingredient is repetition. It effectively tells the brain that "I keep saying this, so it must be important," and each repetition strengthens the neural connection.

Lastly, emotion acts as a powerful glue for forming long-term memories. For example, if a friend casually mentions they had a sandwich for lunch, you're likely to forget it immediately. But if they tell you they just witnessed your partner sharing an intimate laugh with someone really attractive, that memory will likely stick with you.

Phew, that was a lot to take in!

Now might be a good time to take a nap and sleep on it.

Puns aside, sleep is essential for memory and learning—it's when your brain processes and consolidates everything you've absorbed. Not only does getting enough rest help you process new information while awake, but memories are consolidated during both **non-rapid eye movement (NREM)** and **rapid eye movement (REM)** phases of the sleep cycle.

During this process, the brain filters through memories from the day, deciding what to store and what to discard. Studies by sleep researchers like Dr. Matthew Walker reveal that not getting enough sleep can reduce your learning abilities by as much as 40%. Yikes!

Unfortunately, memories aren't the most accurate representation of what actually happened. This is because the brain doesn't store memories like books in a library; you cannot take a memory off the shelf and expect it to be a replica of what you experienced the previous time you retrieved it.

Memories are reconstructed in a conversation between neurons. And since memories are often emotionally charged, we remember events based on how we perceived them emotionally at the time. To make matters worse, we often fill in the blanks of specific details each time a memory is reconstructed, resulting in the degradation of memory accuracy over time.

Memories can also be contaminated with information after the fact. In a well-known experiment by psychologist **Elizabeth Loftus**, participants were shown footage of a traffic accident. Some participants were asked how fast the cars were going when they hit each other, and others were asked the same question with a subtle change of the word *hit* to *smashed.* A week later, a follow-up question was asked: "Did you see any broken glass?" Those who had been given the word *smashed* were more than twice as likely to say "yes" than those asked using the word *hit.*[55]

Famous events are also notoriously misremembered. Details of events like the assassinations of Dr. Martin Luther King Jr. and John F. Kennedy, the Challenger explosion, or 9/11 are remembered drastically differently from person to person.

Elizabeth Loftus is an American cognitive psychologist renowned for her groundbreaking work on memory, particularly the concept of false memories. Her research demonstrated how memories can be distorted by misinformation and how suggestive questioning can lead to the creation of entirely false memories. Her findings showed that human memory is not as reliable as once thought, and her research has helped shape modern understanding of the malleability of memory.

CURIOUS FACTS ABOUT MEMORY

Long and short term memory peak in our early twenties. Implicit memory remains stable through middle age and can improve with practice.

The most memorable memories are emotional ones or situations that were very different from our expectations.

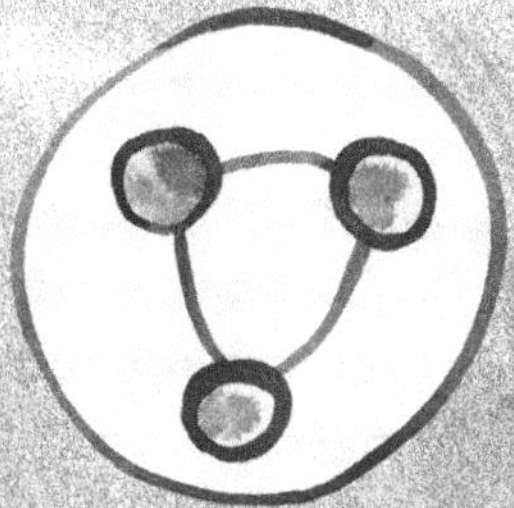

When we retrieve a memory, it activates a neural cluster similar to, but not exactly the same as, the one formed when the memory was first created.

Animals that live longer remember more.

The hippocampus is like the search engine of memory retrieval.

Memories can be personal, collective, or species-based.

Memories can be cumulative. All the times we went to a particular beach blend into one memory.

Telling a story to someone else dramatically increases our memory of it.

Memory is the foundation of imagination. Memory provides the raw materials for thought.

Belief

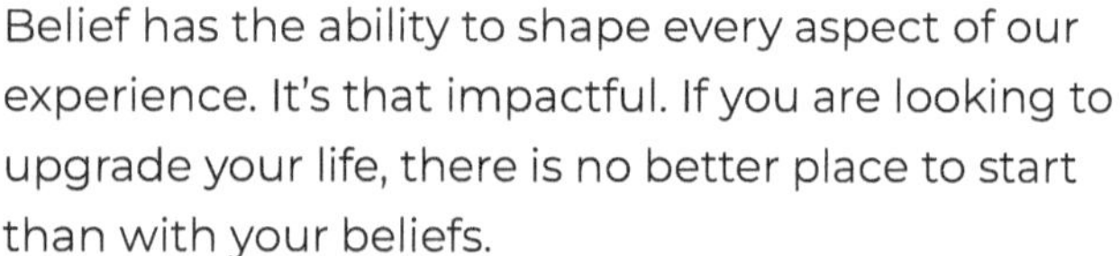

Belief has the ability to shape every aspect of our experience. It's that impactful. If you are looking to upgrade your life, there is no better place to start than with your beliefs.

Our identity, or sense of self, is shaped by our beliefs about who we are. Anything connected to the words "I am" reflects a self-belief. These beliefs drive our habits and behaviors, shaping the way we live.

What many people don't realize is that all their actions, emotional experiences, and perceptions of the world are filtered through their beliefs—most of which operate at a subconscious level. The brain prefers the path of least resistance, and beliefs serve as shortcuts to reduce cognitive load.

For instance, once we believe a friend is trustworthy, we no longer evaluate their intentions every time we interact.

Beliefs can also act as rules we live by to avoid perceived consequences. For example, the belief that "men don't cry" may prevent someone from expressing their emotions.

The key takeaway here is that just because we believe something doesn't mean it's true. What if that trusted friend isn't actually trustworthy? What if we believe we are unlovable or incapable of achieving our goals? These beliefs, true or not, have a profound impact on how we live our lives.

Many of our beliefs, especially those about ourselves, are formed in the first seven years of life. Our brains are still developing at this age, and we are susceptible to misunderstanding the world around us. We are heavily influenced by our culture, religion, and our first relationships—the ones we have with our parents, siblings and primary caregivers.

Before the age of seven, we view the world through an egocentric lens, meaning we're less capable of seeing a situation from someone else's point of view. We believe everything is happening to us and because of us.

Our need to understand why things happen compels us to devise explanations. Some of these explanations are rational and empowering, and sometimes, they are based on a fallacy or a misunderstanding.

The explanations can come from our inner critics, or from those around us. They are fixed in our memory with emotion, which, as you may remember from the previous section, acts as a glue that holds the belief in place. These conclusions stay put and influence us until they are directly addressed. Most of the time, they stay with us for a lifetime and seem to be "just the way things are."

Suppose you grew up in a home where your parents constantly fought and projected their frustration or sadness onto you. You likely believed that you did something wrong or that your parents didn't love you. You just didn't have the capacity to understand the complexity of adult relationships, so you took their behavior and moods personally. Over time, you might have started to believe "I'm unimportant," "Everything is my fault," or "I'm not enough." These are examples of core limiting beliefs.

COMMON CORE LIMITING BELIEFS

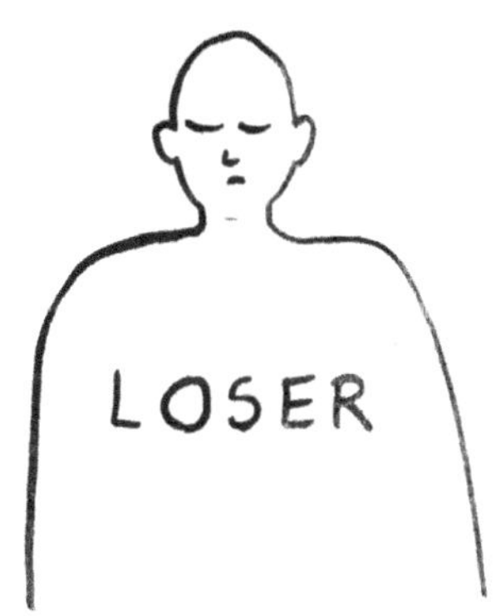

UNWORTHY
I'm a loser. I'm a failure.
I'm broken. I'm stupid.

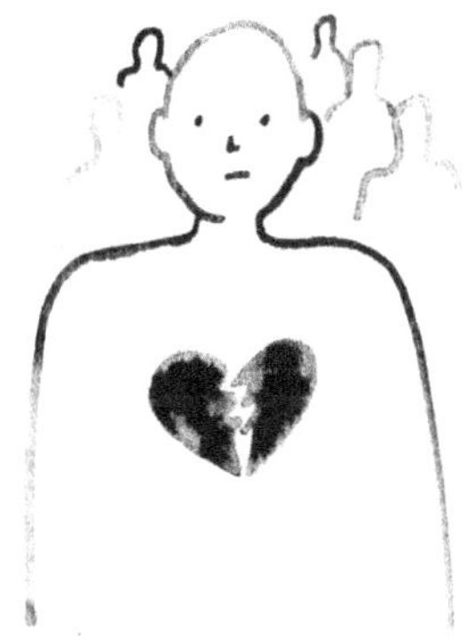

UNLOVABLE
I'll always be alone. No one can
understand me. Nobody likes me.

UNSAFE
I'm in danger.
I can't handle this. I'm weak.

Core beliefs are the very essence of how we see ourselves, others, and the world. They are deeply held assumptions that profoundly influence our thoughts and behaviors.

Our core beliefs can be negative or positive, depending on our early influences in life. For example, if you are scolded and made to feel stupid every time you make a mistake, you might form a belief that failure is unacceptable and develop a fear of trying new things.

Instead, what if you were taught a more thoughtful growth-centered approach that views failure as the first step toward success? This perspective would prompt you to look for areas of improvement and try again. With this mindset, you are likely to believe you can achieve anything with learning and effort.

Can you see how these two different beliefs could lead to two very different life paths and outcomes?

Believing that failure is unacceptable generates negative thoughts when mistakes happen—which they inevitably do—and can lead us to actively avoid trying new things. Many of us become our own worst critics when we make mistakes.

This is just one example of countless limiting beliefs that fuel negative thoughts and emotions. In the example above, the belief and the thoughts it generates simply aren't true. Failure and mistakes are a necessary part of learning and are actually indicators of success and personal growth.

**Stories are like atoms...
the universe is made of them.**

Limiting beliefs can also come packaged in the stories we tell ourselves.
We hold them so deeply that we assume they are true simply because they feel
true to us. They are often self-fulfilling prophecies that reinforce themselves,
further convincing us that they must be true. As in the previous example, if you
believe you will fail when you try new things, you will be stressed and insecure,
leading to failure and reinforcing your belief that you are incompetent. If your
belief is that you are unlovable, you will not be able to express or accept love.
As a result, you may find that you have no loving relationships, which
gives your belief the semblance of being true.

Our beliefs shape our identity and personality. We are who we believe we are.
For example, we may have had an antisocial parent or bad social experiences
at a young age. Over time, we construct the belief that social situations are
uncomfortable, make us nervous, and that we cannot handle them. As a result,
we avoid socializing and label ourselves shy to explain our behavior. This story
becomes part of the collection of stories that we call our personality.

In many cultures, stories are told to convey morals. There are stories about the
perils of succumbing to temptation, the importance of taking care of elders,
and countless other themes linked to human experience. **These stories are
woven into the fabric of our being.**

It's helpful to remember that stories exist to guide us, not to define us. Our
stories are malleable and can be reshaped, especially if they were initially
influenced by events we didn't fully understand at the time. How we interpreted
those events created thought patterns that were woven into us as beliefs.

Some thought patterns may have led to self-imposed limitations, shaping the
choices we make and how we see ourselves. These patterns can leave us feeling
weak, scared, and stuck. When we challenge these patterns, it's natural to feel
discomfort or fear, and we might be tempted to retreat or adapt in ways that
feel protective. We may even create a fictitious self to cope with pain.

For many of us, this false self becomes who we believe we are. It disconnects us from our authentic feelings, needs, and desires, often forming as a response to seeking love and approval from our primary caregivers— a paramount need in early childhood.

Through this self-betrayal, we internalize the belief that the emotional world of others is more important than our own. As a result, we may not learn how to regulate our emotions, communicate our needs, or take actions aligned with our true feelings. Instead, we sacrifice parts of ourselves to create a sense of safety and acceptance.

By examining and reframing limiting beliefs, we can transform our self-image. Rather than feeling stuck or disempowered, we can rediscover ourselves as capable, conscious creators of our lives.

What's the most important takeaway of this section? **Just because we believe the stories we tell ourselves doesn't mean they are true.** In fact, throughout history, many things people believed to be true were eventually overturned in dramatic fashion.

With refocused awareness, we can question our beliefs and thought patterns to determine whether they are true and beneficial to us. One of the most powerful ways to evolve and return to our authentic selves is to identify untrue beliefs and understand that we have the power to release them.

> *Hint…If you feel bad while thinking a particular thought, in one way or another, that thought is likely untrue. Follow its trail and you can identify the underlying limiting belief it stems from.*

Once we release a limiting belief through a transformative process, we can use new evidence to create helpful beliefs that generate positive, empowering thoughts. This is how we change our minds and, ultimately, our lives. Your habits of thinking and imagining mold your destiny.

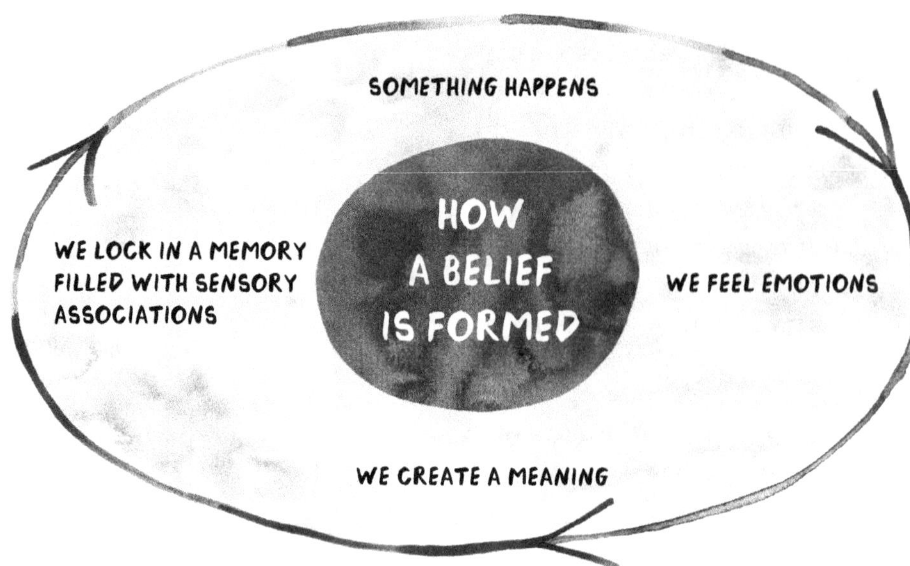

The Power of Belief in a Pill

Did you know that many medications work largely because we believe they will? The placebo effect isn't just a fluke—it's a window into the mind's ability to influence the body. For example, in the U.S., baby aspirin is commonly used to prevent heart disease.

But studies show it offers no measurable benefit to people in the U.K. The difference? Not the drug—it's the expectation. Our beliefs literally shape our biology.

Medicines and Healthcare Products Regulatory Agency. "Aspirin Not Licensed for Primary Prevention of Thrombotic Vascular Disease." GOV.UK. 3 Oct 2009.

https://www.gov.uk/drug-safety-update/aspirin-not-licensed-for-primary-prevention-of-thrombotic-vascular-disease

---

Let's talk about the placebo effect for a moment. This phenomenon occurs when someone is given a treatment with no active remedial properties, yet their symptoms improve.

Belief plays a tremendous role here. Beliefs create thoughts, thoughts create emotions, and these emotions affect our body through neurochemical signals and hormones. Therefore, what we believe has a tangible, physical impact on our bodies and health.

One reason placebos are effective is that many diseases can result from, or be exacerbated by, negative states produced from fear and stress.

Placebos change the stories we tell ourselves.

Simply believing that we've received a beneficial treatment positively affects our behavior and can even cause the release of brain chemicals, like endorphins, that aid in relieving and resolving symptoms.

Just as the mind can cause physical disorders, it can also provide the cure. The law of belief is the law of life: unite mentally and emotionally with your intentions, embody them, and they will, more often than not, come to pass.

Emotion

When life feels like a roller coaster ride, it's our emotions driving the ups and downs. The contrast between the highs and lows infuses our existence with energy, meaning, and variety.

Emotions influence every aspect of our lives, from our relationships and memory to our decision-making and health. They are the chemical signatures of our experiences, shaped by our thoughts and the meanings we've assigned to those experiences. Emotions manifest as brain chemicals that flow through our bodies.

Deeply linked to our beliefs, emotions reinforce our convictions, making them difficult to change. This is why challenging and altering our beliefs can be tricky; our emotions seem to validate our beliefs, leading us to dismiss alternative perspectives that may exist.

Negative emotions narrow our focus and limit our ability to see the broader truth. When we are fearful or angry, our minds become hyper-focused on these negative emotions because they evolved primarily to keep us alive in dangerous situations. The result is tunnel vision, a high degree of attention and focus on the unwanted thing we are experiencing.

WHAT ARE MY EMOTIONS TELLING ME?

Anger is a clue that our boundaries have been crossed and that we may have to defend ourselves against something.

Jealousy is inviting us to get clarity on what we really want and to develop our potential.

Sadness is an invitation to find out where we have unmet expectations, are out of alignment, or are feeling drained.

Guilt is asking what needs to be corrected or made right.

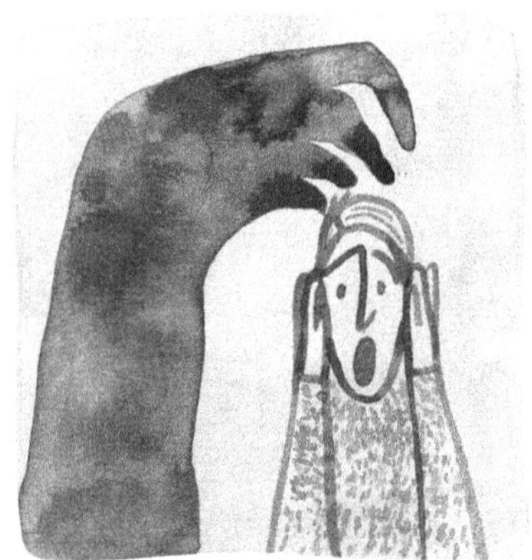

Fear is a message to prepare.

On the other hand, **positive emotions expand our focus.** They bond us socially, calm the nervous system, and encourage future planning and creativity.

We feel emotions as physical sensations in the body. Emotions and bodily sensations are intricately intertwined in a bidirectional network, where each can influence the other. Understanding our feelings is an essential part of emotional intelligence.

Emotional intelligence is the ability to positively perceive, understand, and manage our emotions and the emotions of others. This allows us to relieve stress, overcome challenges, empathize with others, communicate effectively, and resolve conflict.

In addition to expressing our emotions, identifying and labelling them is an important step on the path to integrating them.

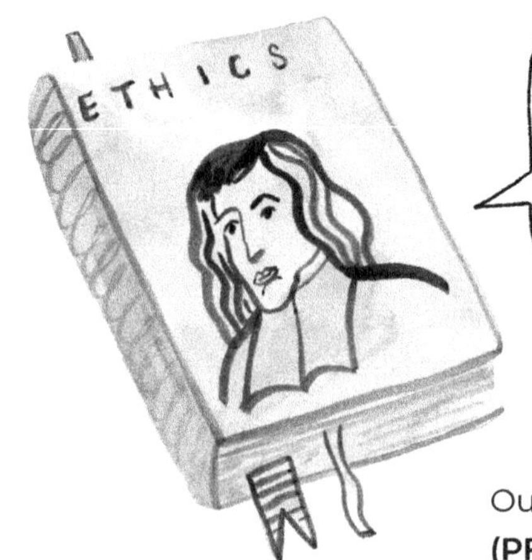

Without emotional intelligence, we fall victim to our emotions. We become addicted to the chemicals produced in response to our thoughts. Our emotions can spiral out of control, trapping us and causing needless distress.

Our brains have circuits from the limbic region to the **prefrontal cortex (PFC).** Signals of intense emotion can create neural static, sabotaging the ability of the PFC to maintain working memory. We all know how challenging it can be to think straight when we are upset. And this is why **continual emotional distress can create deficits in our intellectual abilities, crippling our learning capacity.**

Emotional momentum: When we feel happy, we are most likely to learn better, recall pleasant memories, and have happier thoughts arise. When we feel upset, the reverse occurs.

Emotional contagion: When we are exposed to negative emotion, especially when it is prolonged, we start to feel more negative ourselves. That's why it's important to enter an emotionally charged situation with emotional boundaries—and a clear understanding that joining the pity party or rage-fest won't help anyone!

Prolonged emotional distress or profoundly overwhelming events can result in trauma. Trauma causes an overload in the mind that is difficult to process and integrate. As a result, considerable mental energy is spent trying to make sense of painful situations. There are no objective criteria to determine which events will cause **trauma,** as it's **defined more by the emotional response than by the trigger itself.**

Unprocessed trauma causes distorted perceptions of ourselves and the world. We may come to believe we aren't safe, we don't deserve love, or that we can't have what we need.

The mind will repress or dissociate from painful memories to defend itself against the overwhelming emotions that arise. Our brilliant mind tries to help us cope by setting up defense mechanisms. Although they are meant to protect us, these defense mechanisms interfere with our choices and negatively affect our relationships, career, and ability to thrive and be happy.

They can manifest as: seeking numbing distractions such as addictions, zoning out or experiencing dissociation, exhibiting hair-trigger aggression, or avoiding of human connection, to name just a few.

Repressed emotions still have the power to affect us. When we refuse to feel and process our emotions, they are moved to unconscious territory, where they become more powerful and primitive. What we fail to deal with becomes part of our shadow, negatively impacting our behavior and health.

TYPES OF DEFENSES

REPRESSION

Repression is a motivated "forgetting" of a situation in which we become unaware of what we are reacting to.

Repressed emotions change form. Anger can turn into passive aggression or apathy. Fear often becomes confusion or anxiety. Sadness can turn into anger, guilt or shame. Shame can manifest as grandiosity.

DENIAL

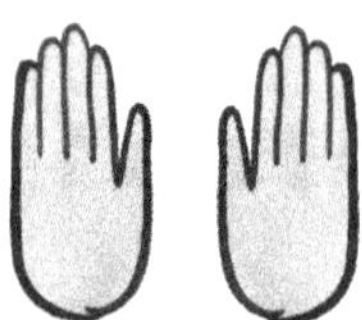

Denial is the refusal or inability to accept the truth of a situation. Statements of denial include: "This isn't happening" and "It's not so bad." Denial prevents us from confronting and addressing the reality of our circumstances.

PROJECTION

Projection is accurately represented by the statement "If you spot it, you got it."

Rather than facing our negative traits, we see the negative qualities in others. If you react to it, it's in you, waiting to be healed.

RATIONALIZATION

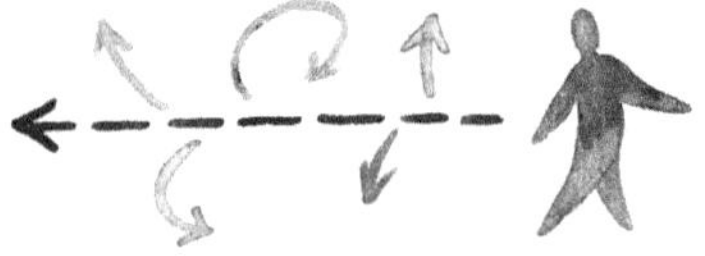

Rationalization is an anti-responsibility mechanism that allows us to justify or explain what we'd rather not face or admit. Rationalization effectively interferes with our ability to learn the lessons that are available to us.

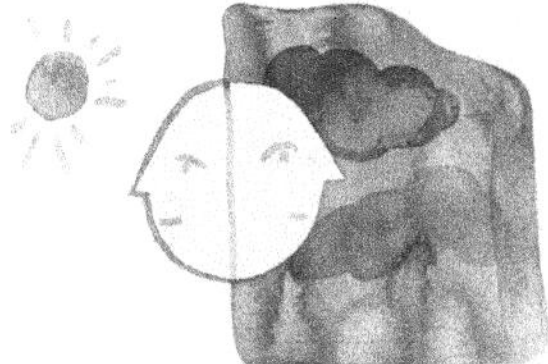

SPLITTING

Splitting involves black-and-white thinking that oversimplifies complex situations to avoid the effort of nuanced thought. It manifests as idealizing or demonizing people or situations.

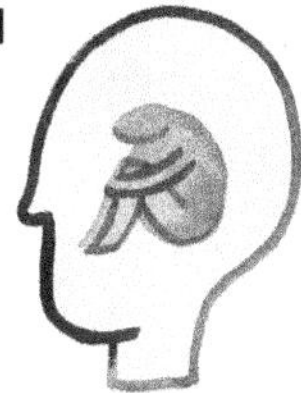

INTELLECTUALIZATION

Intellectualization involves focusing on abstract details to sidestep emotional stress. By fixating on reasoning, we distance ourselves from our emotions, choosing to "live in our heads."

DISASSOCIATION

Dissociation involves disconnecting from our thoughts, feelings, memories, or identity to manage trauma or stress. Escaping or numbing behaviors, including compulsive addictions, are used to fill unconscious voids.

Inspired by the foundational work of Anna and Sigmund Freud, who first mapped the mind's elegant instinct to protect through subconscious defense mechanisms.

The good news is that there are ways to identify and heal these wounds. Negative emotions provide a trail of breadcrumbs that our minds can follow to discover the root cause of our beliefs, often originating from childhood experiences.

The starting point of the breadcrumbs is a story that we are telling ourselves. Through awareness, we can evaluate whether these stories are true or based on beliefs that no longer serve us. We may then release the emotions these stories cause and create new meanings for our experiences.

Intuition

The Yoruba Concept of Ori:
In Yoruba spirituality, Ori is considered the personal deity or spiritual head that guides an individual's destiny and consciousness. Ori represents both a person's inner mind and their spiritual guide, holding the wisdom and knowledge necessary for a fulfilled life. Aligning with one's Ori brings success and harmony. Ori is often invoked in prayers and rituals for clarity and mental fortitude.

Albert Einstein also said that he would sometimes feel certain he was right about something without having a logical reason for his gut feeling.[62] Many scientists might agree that much of scientific discovery and innovation starts with intuition.

A heightened sense of awareness. Whispers from our souls. That immediate "yes" recognition. Our gut feelings. Intuition is known in many ways and is hard to elucidate.

Defined as the power or faculty of attaining knowledge or cognition without evident rational thought and inference, intuition provides a bridge between our conscious and subconscious minds.

Some people see intuition as a link to our higher selves or universal wisdom, while others view it as a function of the autonomic nervous system. Perhaps it's both. Whatever its origin, intuition helps us ask meaningful questions in our search for truth and guides us in uncovering deeper insights within the rich tapestry of our experiences.

Our intuition acts like a messenger from our subconscious mind, providing us with answers before we fully rationalize a situation. This happens because the subconscious mind absorbs millions of bits of sensory data every second through our nervous system and processes it in a complex, non-linear way that our conscious mind isn't involved in. It looks for patterns and connections that we are not consciously aware of. Because of this, we're only aware of a tiny fraction of what we're processing, which makes our gut feelings seem quite mysterious.

Intuitive thinking can be thought of as a process of perceiving, feeling, and instinctive understanding.

Perceiving involves sensing and observing; its how we use our senses to become aware of our surroundings and how our bodies react to them.

Feeling is connecting with what we perceive and experiencing the emotions that arise in our bodies.

Instinctive understanding occurs when we've rapidly processed our feelings without any need for conscious reasoning—we just know.

Contrary to intuitive thinking, reflective thinking involves examining our instincts and exploring alternative possibilities. Both are crucial to thoroughly evaluate our decisions.

When faced with a threat or an exciting opportunity, our instincts kick in. Instincts are hardwired into our biology, and they drive our behavior. You can think of instincts as the underlying programming and code that equips us to survive and function as a species.

In addition to the fight-or-flight response, we have several other instincts such as the maternal instinct, fear, curiosity, and comfort, to name just a few. Our gut feelings, often rooted in fear, stem from our subconscious mind processing vast amounts of sensory data without our conscious awareness.

"SECOND BRAIN" ENTERIC NERVOUS SYSTEM

The Enteric Nervous System, often referred to as our Second Brain, is a web of more than 100 million neurons that spans our entire digestive tract. It is capable of operating independent of the brain and spinal cord and produces large amounts of the same neurotransmitters as the brain, such as dopamine and serotonin.

As a social species, we have a strong survival instinct that makes us want to return to the tribe for acceptance and safety. Our pull toward conformity is strong.

Following a path that aligns with our unique interests and values often means going against the status quo. This requires being okay with being misunderstood or even shunned, which can be exceptionally uncomfortable—as it violates the survival instinct that compels us to fit in. Building a strong and healthy sense of self and developing our intuition is invaluable in living an authentic life.

Questioning our fears and the narratives that arise from them requires immense courage and it also brings tremendous rewards. Choosing to elevate our consciousness and honor our uniqueness demands that we forge a deeper relationship with our intuition.

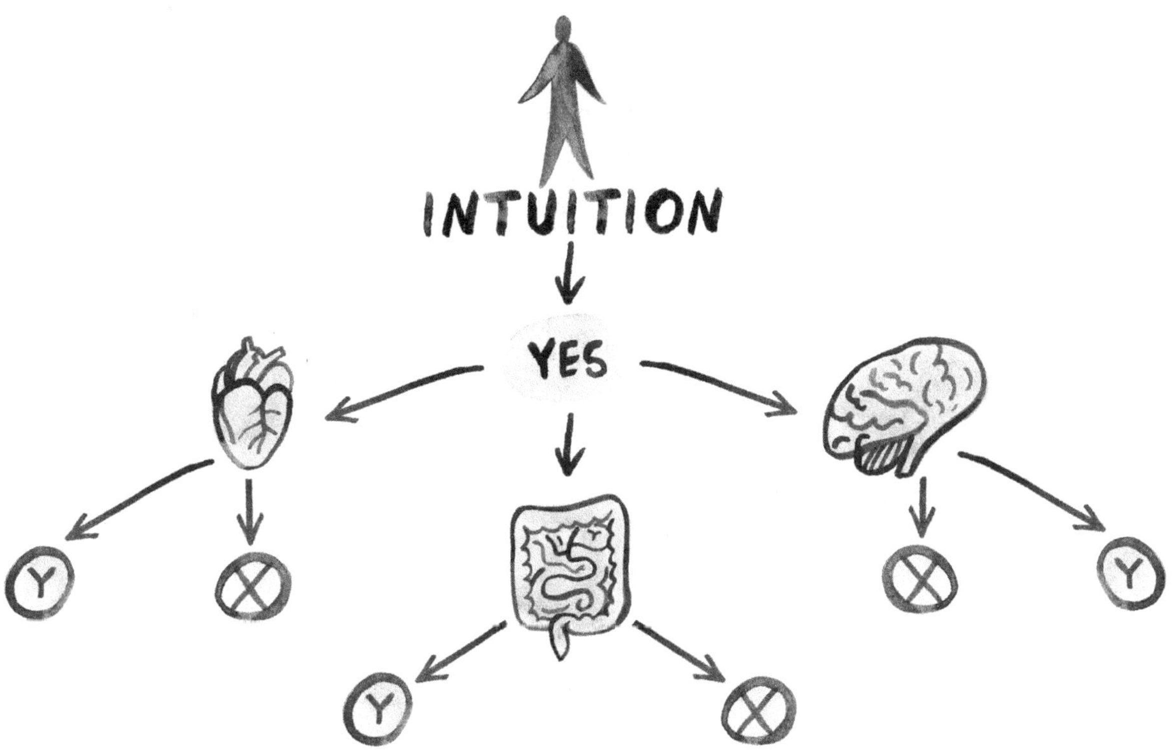

When calling upon your intuition, you may feel a full-body "yes."

If not, notice the signals coming from your head, heart, and gut. Pay attention to any subtle "no"— a tightening, a drop, a sinking wave—and explore what those sensations are trying to tell you.

Choosing the safe path, seduced by comfort or status, traps us into living according to other people's values rather than following our own inner guidance. Once we settle into our comfort zone, we become numb and suppress the very instincts that encourage us to pursue our inner truth.

Intuition is ancient and instinctual—but it is not *always* right.

Intuition is susceptible to cognitive biases, which are systematic errors in our judgment that happen unconsciously. An example of this is confirmation bias, in which we tend to seek, interpret, and recall information that supports our existing beliefs and values.

Despite its potential for error, listening to our intuition provides opportunities to gain deeper insight into our selves, our creativity, and our path forward. It allows us to make decisions based on the collected wisdom of our full experience— even experiences we have forgotten.

Considered the center of the ancient world, Delphi, nestled on the slopes of Mount Parnassus in Greece, has long been associated with the Oracle—one of the most influential women of the classical era.

Authors who mention the Oracle include Aristotle, Euripides, Herodotus, Ovid, Plato, Plutarch, and Sophocles.

Before offering her prophetic counsel, the high priestess followed a sacred ritual. She would bathe in a nearby spring hidden in the woods, walk through the cedar trees, and pass through a dark underground tunnel leading to the entrance of Apollo's temple amphitheater.

She would ascend to the stage and sit on a tripod positioned over a cauldron—Apollo's symbol of prophecy.

Imagination

Derived from the Latin word imago, meaning "image," imagination is the cornerstone of human progress. It has driven the invention of everything from the stone wheel to the smartphone.

Archaeological discoveries reveal that expressions of creativity have been part of our history for a very long time. For example, a 51,000-year-old bone carving was discovered in Germany, and paintings and hand stencils have been found in Indonesia and Spain, dating back more than 40,000 years.

Cave paintings are a testament to early human imagination, showcasing abstract and symbolic thinking through depictions of animals, human figures, and abstract patterns. These ancient artworks often go beyond literal representation, incorporating symbols and creative expressions that suggest deeper meanings, ritualistic uses, and mythological beliefs. Representations like half-human, half-animal hybrids and hunting scenes highlight imaginative myths, religious thoughts, and mental preparations, reflecting early humans' exploration of identity and their ability to project into hypothetical scenarios.

Imagination is to the future what memory is to the past—and they are linked. Our ability to generate mental imagery is not solely dependent on what we can see, hear, feel, taste, or touch in the moment. Rather, it comes from within our mind and is often unconsciously influenced by memories and emotions.

Through imagination we can explore things that aren't physically present, ranging from the familiar (sipping on that latte) to the not-yet-experienced (floating in space).

The subconscious mind loves stories, analogies, and imagery that help us make sense of our reality. Such stories make information more memorable.

In ancient Greece, it was believed that kings and poets received their powers of persuasion from **the Titaness Mnemosyne**, the goddess of memory. Mnemosyne was the daughter of Uranus and Gaia and she was the mother of the Nine Muses, the creativity-inspiring goddesses of science, literature, and the arts.

Even the ancient Greeks knew that creative thinking and imagination were a product of memory. Modern research agrees and gives us insight into how these cognitive processes are connected. Such research shows that the hippocampus comes online both during episodic memory retrieval and imagining future events.[65]

People with a damaged hippocampus who have difficulty recalling their own experiences also show both a diminished ability to imagine the future and a decreased ability to think creatively.

In neural imaging studies where people are asked to imagine a scenario that hasn't happened, the **Default Mode Network (DMN)** comes online. The DMN is a large-scale brain network containing several brain regions that are activated when remembering past experiences. Because it is often active when the mind is wandering in a state of wakeful rest, some people refer to it as the "Imagination Network."

Mnemosyne

Smartphones and technology can reduce our ability to think creatively. The Default Mode Network activates when we focus internally rather than externally. Unfortunately, we often spend our downtime glued to our phones and computers. This valuable downtime could be spent reflecting on the past and envisioning the future, rather than being consumed by trivial posts that contribute little to our personal growth.

Stress, anxiety, and trauma can also impair our ability to be imaginative. Constant and intense stress can cause damage to the hippocampus, which is why people with PTSD frequently experience memory-related difficulties.

Anxiety leads us to fix our imagination on unfavorable future outcomes, making us feel more anxious, thus feeding the cycle. When we are hyperfocused on the negative, we don't have room for divergent, creative thinking.

What is fascinating is that our brains don't always manage to distinguish between imagination and reality. Researchers illustrated this phenomenon in a study that required one group of people to play a simple sequence of piano notes for five days in a row while another group only imagined playing the notes. Each day, the brain region connected to the finger muscles was scanned, and the scans of both groups showed nearly the same number of changes in the brain![66]

This cycle is also what drives anxiety and allows negative thoughts to impact us adversely. When we imagine catastrophic scenarios, we effectively flood our bodies with the stress hormone cortisol. This increases our stress and triggers more negative thinking. Learning to interrupt and break this cycle is crucial for managing anxiety and stress.

The good news is that we can **leverage the power of imagination through visualization.** By vividly rehearsing our desired outcomes and imagining our future selves, we give our mind a clear path toward achieving our goals.

Many artists, inventors, and professional athletes attribute their success to visualization.

Nikola Tesla had an impressive ability to work with models and inventions in his head in 3D. He'd turn them over, pull apart the pieces, and reconfigure them— all in the workshop of his mind.

Imagination is a powerful force, capable of altering our mood, nervous system, and future trajectory—for better or worse. Understanding how imagination works enables us to use it to our advantage rather than to our detriment.

Dreams

The Lakota Concept of Wakan Tanka: In Lakota spirituality, Wakan Tanka refers to the Great Spirit or the Sacred Mystery, which governs all life. The mind is seen as a bridge between the physical world and the spiritual realm. Dreams, visions, and meditative states are crucial for accessing knowledge and guidance from Wakan Tanka. The concept of the mind is deeply connected to intuition and the ability to connect with universal wisdom.

No doubt you've been bewildered by your dreams before—probably quite often.

"Why was I in my grandma's house, except it was in another country somehow, and that random girl I met at the museum was…riding a dragon?"

Dreams have long mystified scientists and theories about their purpose vary widely. Some suggest that dreams are involved in memory consolidation, emotional processing, and rehearsing for potential danger, while others believe they are simply a by-product of our evolution—with no purpose at all.

Studies by neuroscientists seem to confirm at least two benefits of dreaming. Dreams function as a sort of overnight therapy session that enhances creativity and problem-solving.[67]

The molecule noradrenaline is a stress-inducing neurotransmitter most notably present during the fight-or-flight response. Our brain is entirely devoid of this molecule while in REM sleep. At the same time, major emotional and memory areas of the brain come online as we dream. This allows our brains to revisit and reprocess emotionally challenging memories in a calm, safe environment.[68]

Many creative ideas have been attributed to dreams, from the Beatles' song "Yesterday" to Dmitri Mendeleev's periodic table of elements, and even the cultural staple we all use: Google.[69]

During REM sleep, when we dream, the brain processes vast amounts of acquired knowledge and memories, merging them in abstract and innovative ways. This integration helps identify connections between different types of stored information, fostering a mindset that can discover solutions to previously unsolvable problems.

REM Realms: The Science and Soul of Dreaming

Your Mind Never Sleeps: During REM, your brain lights up with activity rivaling your waking hours. Dreaming isn't rest; it's deep inner work.

Everyone Dreams: Whether you remember them or not, dreams are a nightly voyage your subconscious takes—your inner world always whispering.

Even Animals Dream: From your dog twitching in its sleep to birds in quiet slumber, dreaming bridges species.

Training for the Unexpected: Some dreams rehearse danger, running subconscious simulations so you're more prepared for real-life challenges.

When the Body Stays Still but the Mind Wakes: Sleep paralysis is a bizarre liminal state where your body remains frozen, still caught in REM, while your awareness returns—an eerie, powerful moment between worlds.

Colorful Minds, Colorful Dreams: Most people dream in color, but those exposed only to black-and-white media once dreamed in monochrome. Your dream palette may reflect your environment.

Dreams as Early Messengers: Changes in your dreamscape may signal deeper shifts, sometimes even the early signs of neurodegenerative conditions. Your subconscious is always speaking.

THE ASCLEPIONS

The theory of dreams as a form of healing is nothing new. The Asclepions were ancient Greek sanctuaries dedicated to Asclepius, the god of medicine, serving as centers for both spiritual and physical restoration. Set amidst awe-inspiring natural beauty, these sanctuaries created an environment designed for reflection, renewal, and inner clarity.

The healing journey began with Katharsis—a ritual purification involving cleansing baths, fasting, and spiritual preparation. After this, supplicants would offer representations of afflicted body parts or toss coins into sacred springs as tokens of devotion.

They then entered the Abaton, a dream-incubation chamber, seeking revelatory visions from Asclepius. The god often appeared in dreams in the form of his totem animals—the dog, the rooster, or the snake—delivering guidance or direct healing. Priest-physicians trained in dream interpretation would prescribe treatments based on these visions, blending spiritual insight with early medical practice. It was a holistic approach that honored both the symbolic and physical aspects of healing.

One of the most intriguing types of dreams is called lucid dreaming, which occurs when you become aware that you are dreaming while still in the dream. Often the dreamer gains some control over the actions, characters, and narratives in the dream, sort of like being the director of a movie.

There are various techniques for increasing the likelihood of having a lucid dream. One of the most powerful is journaling your dreams each morning. This helps you identify "dream signs"—recurring people, objects, or situations that often appear in your dreams. The more familiar you become with these signs, the easier it becomes to recognize when you're dreaming.

Another effective method is doing frequent reality checks throughout your waking life, until they become second nature. For example, ask yourself, "Am I dreaming?" several times a day while looking at your hands, reading a line of text twice, or trying to push a finger through your opposite palm. In dreams, these simple tests often behave strangely, making you aware that you're dreaming. Over time, these habits carry over into your dreams, allowing you to become lucid when you notice something's off.

But it's not just in our dreams that we create our reality...

Reality Creation

Not to cause an existential crisis, but what is reality?

Well, there is objective reality—everything that exists in our physical universe, even beyond our perception, including radio waves and black holes. We know these phenomena are there, but we can't perceive them without the help of technology.

CYMATICS

Salt dances on a speaker, forming intricate patterns that reveal the hidden geometry of sound waves. This phenomenon, known as cymatics, visually captures the wave vibrations shaping the physical world.

On a trembling surface, salt blooms into patterns—sound made visible, vibration made art. And as the frequency rises, the patterns grow more complex, more beautiful, more refined.

Your voice works the same magic. Its frequency ripples through your body, coaxing your cells into new choreography—shifting shape in response to the words and tone you choose.

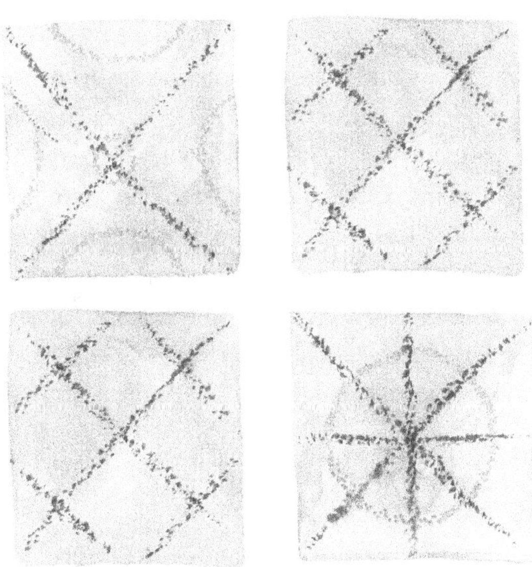

Then there is our perceived human reality, the limited way we experience objective reality through our senses. This is the reality we experience collectively as a species, encompassing what we can see, smell, hear, taste, and touch.

And there is also our personal subjective reality—the way we perceive the world through our individual bodies, beliefs, and life experiences. Our subjective reality is influenced to a large degree by where we live, our families, and our education. Reality varies greatly from person to person and, as anyone who has traveled to another country may verify, from culture to culture as well.

Time seems to move slower for those who wait.

The reality (heh heh) is that we mix and dabble in all of these realities at any given time during our waking hours. In half a second, the brain takes in information, sifts it to find patterns, and uses it to build a multi-sensory technicolor show that we experience as life.

However, we typically experience only a tiny slice of reality. In order to prevent the brain from being overwhelmed by a constant deluge of sensory input, we need some sort of filtering system so that we can pay attention to what our body and mind identify as the most important information at that time.

This filtering system is called the **Reticular Activating System (RAS).** The RAS is a collection of brain areas that queue up neuromodulators in response to data received by the ears, and predominantly, the eyes. The main neuromodulators are serotonin (associated with contentment and gratitude), dopamine (associated with desire and motivation), acetylcholine (associated with focus), and epinephrine (associated with alertness). You can think of the RAS as a template for focusing on ideas, information, or goals you deem important. When you perceive something in your environment that relates to that template, the RAS queues up the appropriate neuromodulator, increases your perception and arousal, and either contracts or dilates your focus. What we regard as important can be intentional, like setting a personal goal, or a product of our memories, beliefs, or fears.

We don't respond to reality itself, but to a map of reality—a version filtered through our beliefs, past experiences, values, and personality. This inner map is shaped by generalizations, distortions, and omissions based on what our subconscious deems relevant. Our expectations play a powerful role in shaping what we perceive. In fact, the brain may even "bend the rules" to align reality with what it expects to be true. It doesn't like to be wrong.

Consider the illusion of solidity. Objects that seem stable and fixed are actually made of vibrating energy and constantly moving information. In truth, everything is in flux. While knowing this may not change how we physically experience the world, it reminds us that appearances can deceive—and that what we believe to be real is not always the whole truth.

Speaking of truth and the truth of reality...

Philosophers throughout history have contemplated the nature of the mind and its relationship to the body and the world.

An Ionian Greek philosopher and mathematician, **Pythagoras** believed that at the deepest level, reality is mathematical in nature. He sought to decipher the code by which reality is structured, exploring the idea that numbers and their relationships underpin the very fabric of existence.

Another belief attributed to Pythagoras was that of *musica universalis* or "harmony of the spheres." According to this belief, the movement of the planets and stars can be reduced to mathematical ratios that correspond with musical notes, thereby creating an inaudible musical symphony.

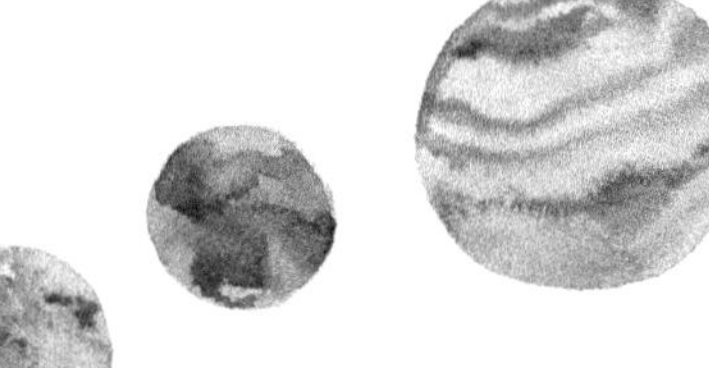

Pythagoras

Pythagoras taught that "the seven Muses" of Greek mythology were actually the seven planets singing together.

Pythagoras 570–490 BCE

Heraclitus

Little is known about the life of **Heraclitus.** He wrote a single work, of which only fragments have survived, thanks to those who cited him. The central idea of his philosophy is the **unity in opposites**, which maintains that the existence or identity of an entity depends on the co-existence of its opposite. They are interconnected and interdependent.

For example, up cannot exist without down, nor day without night. Heraclitus saw the world as being in a constant state of flux, ever-changing as it stays the same, such as dry becoming wet, hot becoming cold, and on and on.

An inhabitant of Athens, in Ancient Greece, **Socrates** is generally considered the founder of Western philosophy, and was one of the earliest philosophers of the ethical tradition of thought. He introduced the Socratic method, an argumentative dialogue between two individuals that uses short questions and answers to stimulate critical thinking and uncover presuppositions, which are built-in beliefs or ideas. Socrates is famous for proclaiming his ignorance, suggesting that the first step to philosophical enlightenment is admitting that you know nothing.

Socrates

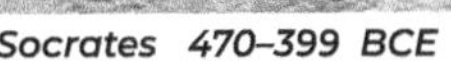

Heraclitus 535–475 BCE

Socrates 470–399 BCE

PLATO'S ALLEGORY OF THE CAVE

Plato was a Greek philosopher during the Classical period of Ancient Greece and is a central figure in the history of philosophy.

He is most famous for his philosophical **theory of Forms** or theory of Ideas. This theory claims that the physical world we perceive is less real as the timeless and absolute world of forms or ideas. Ideas in this sense refer to the non-physical essence of all things—an objective blueprint of the perfection of an object or quality; for example, the form of beauty or the form of a circle. Objects and matter in our physical world are merely manifestations or copies of these forms.

Plato thus suggests the existence of two worlds—a perfect, eternal, and changeless *realm of Being*, beyond space and time, and an ever-changing imperfect *realm of Becoming*.

Platonic solids play a central role in Plato's philosophy. He linked each of the classical elements to a geometric shape, suggesting that these forms symbolized the fundamental nature of the physical world. Earth was represented by the cube, air by the octahedron, water by the icosahedron, and fire by the tetrahedron. These shapes are not only philosophically significant—they are also foundational in the study of geometry, symmetry, and the hidden order of the cosmos.

Plato   428–347 (Approx.) BCE

THE PLATONIC SOLIDS

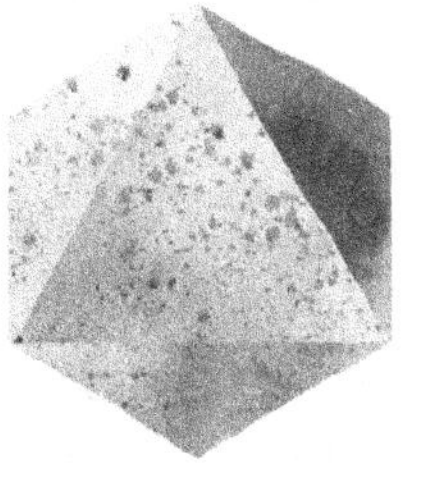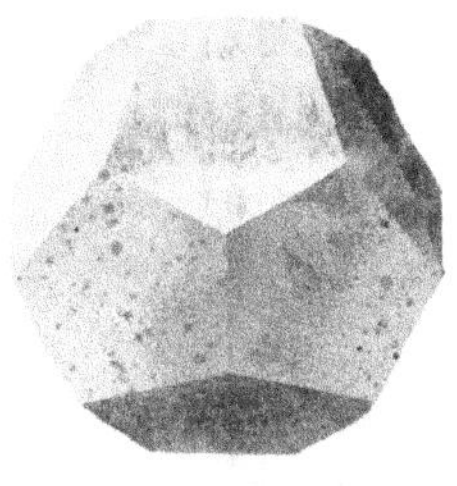

WATER EARTH FIRE AIR AETHER

The **Eleusinian Mysteries** were ancient Greece's most secretive and transformative rituals, offering initiates profound insights into life, death, and the afterlife. Centered on the myth of Demeter and Persephone, they symbolized death and rebirth, promising spiritual awakening and a release from the fear of death. It is speculated that even philosophers like Plato and Socrates attended. Despite lasting nearly 2,000 years, the details remain a mystery, guarded by an unbroken vow of silence.

Leonardo da Vinci

"Everything comes from everything, and everything is made out of everything, and everything returns into everything."[72]

An Italian polymath of the High Renaissance, **Leonardo di ser Piero da Vinci** (say that five times fast!) originally gained fame for his paintings, but also became renowned for his notebooks, which featured drawings and notes on a variety of subjects, including anatomy, botany, and astronomy. Widely considered a genius who embodied the ideals of his time, Leonardo's curiosity and innovation extended beyond art, influencing science and technology in ways that were centuries ahead of his time. His work continues to inspire and fascinate scholars and enthusiasts alike.

STORY INTERLUDE

Lily, a 12-year-old girl, and her concerned parents came into my office one day with a medical situation that was becoming life-threatening.

Lily had recently developed a severe fear of needles, which was interfering with her ability to receive life-preserving treatment. Every month, she needed her medicine delivered intravenously, and the mere thought of the procedure was dreadful for her. Her parents explained that there were days of anxiety leading up to the nurse's visit to their home, and then each time she had to face the needle, her heart raced, and she panicked.

Lily's fear was so intense that her body froze completely whenever the nurse approached her with a needle. Both Lily and the nurse were in a difficult situation. The nurse had visited twice without being able to successfully deliver the medication and she was growing frustrated, and Lily desperately needed her medication.

During our initial session, we did a regression to discover the root cause of Lily's intense emotional distress about needles, which originated from an experience she had overhearing a nurse complaining about her inadequate veins. After releasing that, I explained that she had an exceptionally gifted and magical mind, demonstrated by her ability to create big changes in her body through her thoughts and emotions. If she could harness that power, she could produce positive results as well. This realization marked the beginning of her belief shift.

After that first session in the office, I decided to visit Lily's home to better understand her environment. I discovered that the nurse's frustration and impatience were making the situation worse. The nurse had to work overtime while waiting for Lily, which added to the tension. Things had deteriorated to the point where Lily's veins were collapsing due to the stress, making it impossible to administer the medication even when she forced herself to sit still. It was clear we needed to work with Lily's subconscious mind to help her.

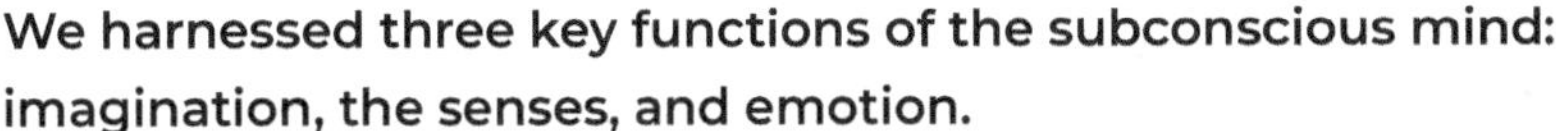

We harnessed three key functions of the subconscious mind: imagination, the senses, and emotion.

In the comfort of Lily's home, we began a transformational session using hypnosis.

First, I redirected Lily's attention and used the power of suggestion to guide her mind toward a serene and symbolic mental image of a river, helping her body relax and improving her blood flow. Next, I utilized a technique that I had developed early in my career called "aroma anchoring" which involves creating an emotional association between hypnotic suggestions and aromatherapy scents. The engagement of her senses provided Lily with a gentle soothing distraction. Once she was calm and steady, I signaled the nurse, who was astounded at how easily she could insert the needle into Lily's vein.

After giving Lily a few more suggestions, she opened her eyes and continued receiving her medication. She felt pride in her achievement.

I took the opportunity to speak with the nurse, explaining what had happened and how she could potentially have a calming and healing effect on her patients in the future. With Lily now relaxed and cooperative, the procedure went smoothly and everyone was thrilled with the outcome.

I gave Lily her aromatherapy inhaler, now anchored to her victory and the hypnotic suggestions, so she could use it for future injections. With her newfound mind-body understanding, she overcame her fear.

This story highlights the mind-body connection. Our subconscious mind, which includes our nervous system and senses, has extraordinary effects on our physical body. By harnessing these subconscious functions, we can guide our bodies back to health.

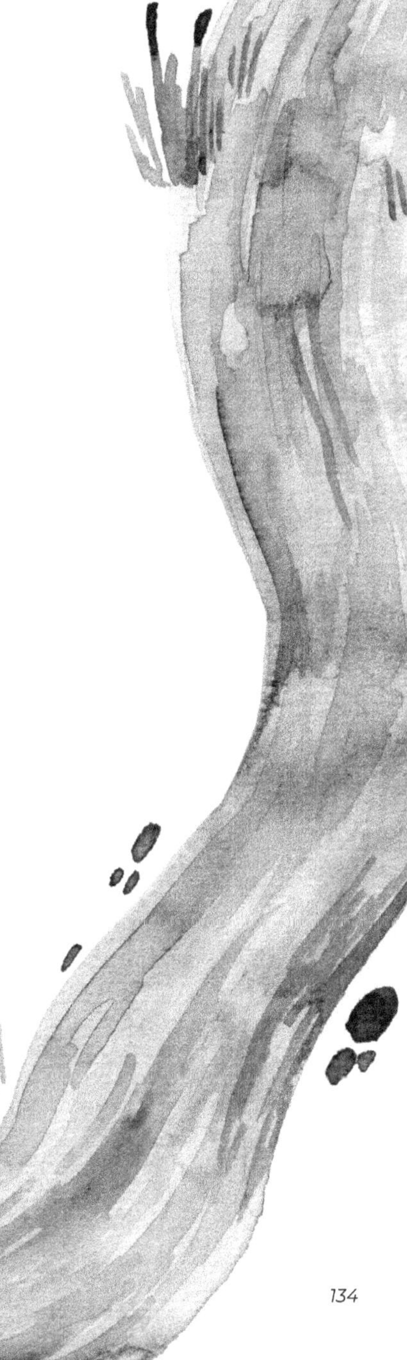

How to Change Your Mind

One of the awe-inspiring features of the mind is the interconnectivity of its functions. Imagination or intuition can trigger autonomic bodily reactions instantly. A certain smell or sound can evoke memories, which then evoke emotion. Emotion acts as a glue that cements beliefs and memories in place.

This interconnectivity can be brilliant when we understand it and feel empowered to direct the mind. However, when misunderstood, this gift can become a curse, leaving us vulnerable to phenomena like anxiety attacks.

A remarkable capacity of the brain is its neuroplasticity. The brain is moldable and capable of rewiring at any stage of life. Previously, it was thought that the brain only changed physically during childhood and adolescence, but we now know that the brain can transform itself throughout our life. This powerful information means that we aren't limited by our current brain function; we can literally change our brain to live healthier and more fulfilling lives.

It's never too late for change with a brilliant mind like yours!

To change, we must be willing to endure temporary discomfort of our ego. When we begin to shift away from familiar ways of being, the ego—which feels separate, alone, and afraid—tries to protect us by rising up in resistance. It clings to the known, even if the known is painful. In addition, people around us may unconsciously pressure us to stay the same, pulling us back into old patterns that serve their own comfort or expectations.

When we bring conscious awareness to these areas, we begin to reprogram the subconscious patterns that once kept us stuck. This is how we move from survival-based looping into aligned, expansive living—creating quantum shifts not through force, but through intentional design.

Addressing four key areas can help us reclaim the reins of the mind, and give us the freedom to choose change:

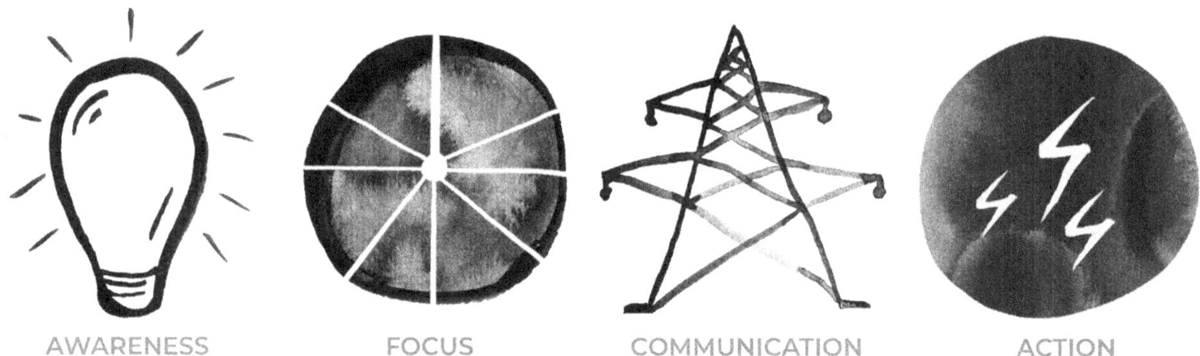

Here is an electrifying analogy to help visualize each of these areas.

Lightbulbs **Illuminate.** They emit omnidirectional waves that **expand** and travel in all directions. This type of light creates the foundation for awareness. As we observe and explore, we illuminate new ways of understanding our patterns, thoughts, emotions, and sensations.

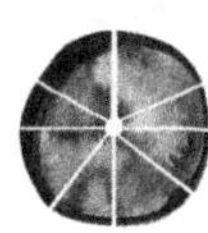

Lasers **Concentrate.** They emit parallel, synchronized waves that **penetrate.** Lasers can perform delicate surgeries as well as cut steel. That's the power of **focus:** when we concentrate our energy on a singular point, task, or goal, we can achieve mighty things.

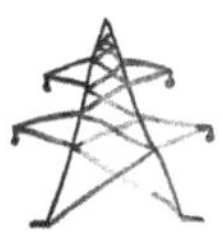

Power Lines **Connect.** A stable connection provides light and warmth to our homes and community. When we integrate all parts of ourselves with loving inner **communication,** we create a strong bond that allows us to navigate our outward relationships with unconditional love and healthy boundaries.

Lightning **Magnetizes.** It strikes with decisive **action.** An inert rock can become magnetized when struck by lightning, which can be hotter than the surface of the sun! Taking action builds momentum and puts us in problem-solving mode, creating a magnetic bond between ourselves and our goals. **This connection also allows us to access a state known as *flow*.**

All types of energy can be beneficial when their specific effects are applied appropriately.

Sometimes we need a soft focus and playful exploration to illuminate possibilities along our path. At other times we need to direct our attention to a single point, like a laser. There are moments when connecting with others, and exploring fresh perspectives is invaluable. And then there are times to take decisive action and stay on task. True power lies in our ability to switch between these modes effortlessly.

Let's break down these four areas further and see how we can utilize them to evolve our minds and achieve our goals.

Awareness

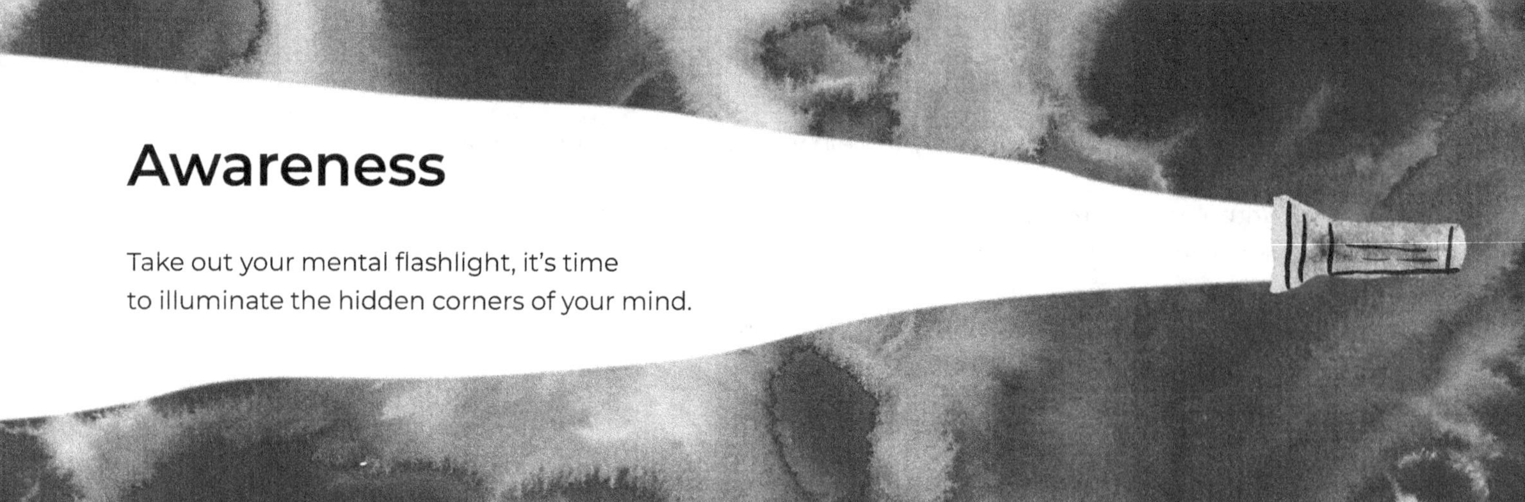

Take out your mental flashlight, it's time
to illuminate the hidden corners of your mind.

Awareness, by definition, is having perception, realization, or knowledge. To change our minds, we must perceive our patterns of thought and emotion, realize what behaviors keep us stuck, and gain knowledge of how our beliefs were formed and how they continue to control us. This is known as self-awareness, which simply means applying awareness to our own experience. When we apply self-awareness to define our purpose, goals, and desires, we create a clear plan for our subconscious mind to follow. This blueprint helps us to automate thoughts and behaviors that support our objectives, making it easier to achieve them.

Self-awareness is the cornerstone of personal development and transformation. After all, if you aren't aware of a problem, how on earth are you going to change it? Awareness allows us to have those "aha!" lightbulb moments in which the pieces start to click together, and we see our patterns and behaviors in a new way.

A lack of awareness keep us stuck.

If we can't identify our patterns, we can't consciously choose to disrupt them. Imagine, for example, that you're struggling with anger, and it's beginning to negatively affect your life. You find yourself regularly lashing out at friends, family members, colleagues, or your employer. Over time, people may begin to distance themselves. Your family may show resentment, and you might even face consequences at work for emotional outbursts. Living in a constant state of anger isn't peaceful or fulfilling—it's a reactive survival state, not anyone's idea of an empowered way to live.

Anger doesn't exist in a vacuum. It often arises when our boundaries are crossed and can serve as a tool to protect and empower us—which can be valuable. However, when anger is disproportionate to the moment, it usually points to deeper, unresolved emotional wounds. These may be old pains that have been reactivated, or a reflection of our difficulty expressing needs and emotions clearly. When we attempt to defend ourselves from perceived threats without awareness, we remain trapped in reactive cycles.

True change only becomes possible when we begin to recognize our triggers and trace them back to their original source.

Learning about the origin of our wounds and beliefs is a powerful way to increase our awareness. Much of our trauma, emotional wounding, and core beliefs are formed during childhood. The reality is that many of us did not grow up in environments where our emotional needs were consistently met, if at all.

Some of us experienced emotional or physical violence at home, or were bullied by peers, or even parents. We may have been told certain emotions were unacceptable, or that we should "man up" We learned to deny parts of who were in order to be loved and accepted by our caregivers.

As a result, we formed beliefs about ourselves and the world based on our parents' beliefs and the behaviors modeled to us.

To change habits and, therefore, the quality of our life, we must start by becoming aware of our beliefs.

Trauma and emotional wounding can occur in many ways, and most of us have experienced them to some degree. These wounds, along with the beliefs we form as a result, follow us and shape our entire lives unless we address and resolve them.

When we fail to fully process our experiences and uncover their lessons, we are left wounded and plagued by triggers that link us to our original pain points and limiting beliefs. Unhealed trauma propels us to make harmful choices.

We can support the healing process by becoming aware of our feelings and triggers and by examining the initial experiences they are connected to. By clearing up misunderstandings and gaining new insights into old memories, we break the cycle and can move in a new direction. Once trauma is processed, the limiting beliefs fall away, and our view of ourselves and the world expands. This is how we heal.

Awareness is a vital step in understanding our emotions. Emotions often show up as physical sensations in the body: our heart rate may increase, we might sweat, tremble, or feel numb or chilled. Anger can feel like heat rising as it boils up from within.

By tuning into how emotions feel in our bodies, we gain insight into when an experience has impacted us emotionally. This awareness also helps us recognize when we've returned to a state of calm and regulation where we can reclaim a grounded sense of presence.

Additionally, our emotions can help us increase our awareness of our thought patterns.

Unproductive thinking leaves emotional clues. For example, when we feel guilt, our minds dwell on self-judgment about the past.

Conversely, feelings of worry involve repetitive fixation on potential negative future outcomes. Both the past and the future are functional illusions because they don't really exist. When we mentally live in the past or the future, we prevent ourselves from experiencing the richness of the present moment—the only moment that truly matters.

Learning to ground ourselves in the present moment and slow the pace of our minds is a powerful practice that opens the path to new possibilities. A busy mind is like a spider web with something trapped inside, twitching and vibrating, pulling our focus in every direction. But through mindfulness and presence, we begin to untangle the chaos. We break free from mental clutter and uncover clarity.

Possibly the most powerful tool we have to ground ourselves in the present moment is our breath. Becoming aware of our breathing connects us to our bodies and anchors us in the *now*. By consciously deepening and slowing our breath, we can calm our nervous system and direct our body to return to a state of rest.

There are many breathwork techniques you can explore for various purposes, including relaxation, focus, and awareness. Yoga and meditation are two richly beneficial practices that can help us connect with our breathing and return to our bodies.

Beyond its meditative benefits, yoga offers considerable value for both mind and body. Physically, yoga can increase your flexibility, muscle strength, respiration, and even your cardiovascular health. Mentally, yoga calms the nervous system and reduces anxiety and stress, while increasing mental clarity and awareness.

Other tools you can use to aid you in changing your mind, mood, and vibe include exercise, music, aromatherapy, cold therapy, and sauna. The key is to try many, notice the effects, and continue those that work for you.

You've probably heard of the term **mindfulness** by now. As a refresher, mindfulness is a state of being in which you focus on becoming intensely aware of the present moment—what you are sensing and feeling—without interpretations or judgments. Mindfulness may seem like a waste of time to a productivity addict, but trust me, you get more important things done with a clear mind. Clearing your mind rearranges your priorities and allows you to observe your thought patterns without judging them. It is a central tool for building awareness.

Bringing awareness to our breathing or other bodily sensations also serves as a helpful interruption when we find ourselves caught in negative thought patterns.

Lao Tzu

# AWARENESS TOOL: MINDFULNESS

Here are some ways to incorporate mindfulness into your day:

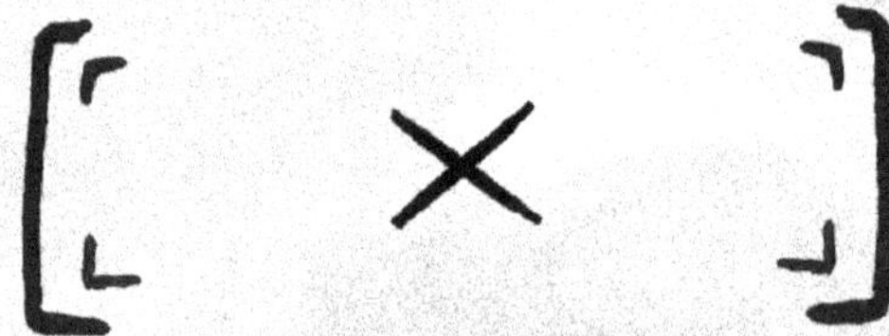

Focus your attention on any activity in which you are engaged in the present moment. This could be walking in nature, eating a meal, listening to music, or even washing the dishes.

Activate your senses: Feel the breeze dance across your skin, smell the wood and earth as you walk through the forest, or actively listen to the birds, crickets, and squirrels.

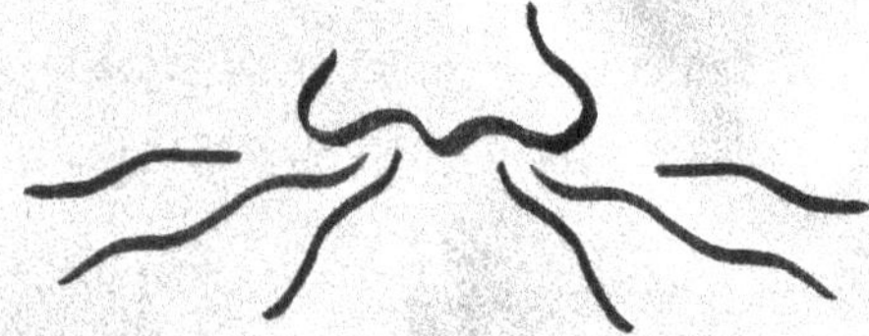

Your breath is an anchor. Pay attention to the sensation of your chest expanding with each breath and the air being inhaled through your nose and exhaled out of your mouth.

JUST FEEL IT

Practice a few minutes at a time throughout your day. Let your thinking mind go, be in the experience of the present moment without judging, analyzing, or predicting—just feel it.

WERE ATTENTION GOES, ENERGY FLOWS.[80]

Cycles

Cycles are a built-in feature of the universe. Everything in the universe has a unique frequency and rhythm, and these different frequencies and rhythms develop into patterns and cycles. The 24-hour day is related to the Earth's rotation and causes a circadian rhythm. The 28-day lunar cycle involves movements of the Earth, Sun, and Moon in relation to each other. These cycles affect our bodies and moods, the migration of animals, the changing of seasons, and the ebb and flow of ocean tides.

What if paying attention to them communicates wisdom to us and helps increase our awareness?

By tuning into these natural rhythms, we gain insights that enhance our understanding of our environment, leading to a more harmonious and balanced life.

Ancient and indigenous cultures have traditionally relied on natural signs to guide their awareness. Messages have been sent and received through the changing seasons, celestial alignments, moon cycles, and totem animals. These cultures understood that nature's rhythms hold valuable insights and wisdom. By observing and aligning with these natural patterns, they were able to make decisions, predict changes, and maintain harmony with their environment. Embracing this wisdom can deepen our connection to the world around us and enhance our awareness in modern life.

Focus

> *"I suppose it is tempting, if the only tool you have is a hammer, to treat everything as if it were a nail."*[82]
>
> **Abraham Maslow**

Playing with your cat using a laser pointer is a good analogy for thinking about focus. The laser is a beam of light focused on a singular point, and the cat is laser-focused on its pursuit of that red dot.

Concentrated attention, or focus, influences all aspects of our mind, body, and relationships. When we focus on something, it takes center stage while everything else recedes into the background.

Focus can be driven by our emotions or willpower; however, willpower has limited control over our emotions, which can take us along for the ride. Mastering our emotions is essential for altering entrenched patterns in our minds.

What we focus on shapes our perspective, which in turn, evokes specific feelings. This is why two people can experience the same event but have fundamentally different emotional reactions. For example, when stuck in a traffic jam, one person might focus on the inconvenience, the incompetence of the other drivers, and how late they'll be, leaving them feeling infuriated.

Another person, accepting the situation as inevitable, might be happy to have extra time to listen to their favorite podcast, or mentally prepare for a meeting, feeling calm and content. The situation hasn't changed, but the focus has.

This illustrates that by changing what you pay attention to, you can physically alter your mind and body. You gain control of your nervous system, stress response, and your emotions.

We face pivotal decisions about where to direct our focus and the meanings we assign to life's events. These choices, which are virtually limitless, ultimately grant us power and freedom in our lives.

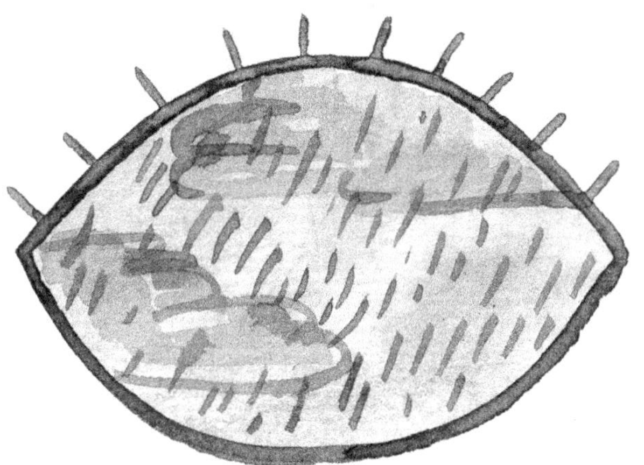

Be cautious of having high expectations. **Unmet expectations often become perceived as problems.** With so much information coming at us, we tend to find whatever we look for, whether negative or positive. When we focus only on the negative and are disappointed by unmet expectations, we are bound to attract more negativity. The good news is, the same goes for positivity.

When we focus on a goal, we are more receptive to perspectives, information, and opportunities that move us toward it. Obsession can lead to faster manifestation because we gain a singular focus, making our entire world revolve around that goal.

Much of what we focus on is habitual. Our evolution trained us to fixate on information relevant to our survival, whether that leads to social acceptance or the avoidance of physical danger. This is why we are experts at pattern recognition. Unfortunately, much of our focus is misguided, fixating on what is missing or what we cannot control.

Our brains toggle between two modes at any given moment: focus and daydreaming. Both are equally important and have clear benefits. Focus helps survive and engage with the world effectively. Less obvious, however, are the benefits of defocusing the mind.

When we're relaxed, the brain activates the default mode network which is a group off interconnected brain regions that become more active when we're chill. In this state, the mind is doing anything but resting; it is activating old memories, traveling between past, present and future, and combining ideas in new ways. **Letting the mind daydream like this can enhance our creativity**—allowing us to reflect inwardly and increasing our levels of self-awareness. It can also lead to "aha" moments in which we can gain clarity and tweak our goals.

Meditation is the most effective way to grow your focus muscle. When a computer freezes or has other inconvenient glitches, what is the most common fix? A restart! Similarly, most of us know that closing open windows on a slow computer improves processing speed and power.

Stilling the mind provides us a reboot that increases our efficiency and mental power. By practicing mental stillness, we move from conscious to subconscious functioning, linking ourselves with the greater mind and giving our prefrontal cortex a break from constant analyzing and predicting.

While the conscious mind analyzes sensory input to determine our reality focusing on our body, environment, and time, the subconscious mind links us with timeless presence. This shift allows for greater mental clarity and cognitive function.

A still mind also provides us with a bird's eye view of our self-talk. By observing this inner dialogue, we can call a cease-fire if it becomes negative or critical, allowing us to realign with our desires instead of merely reacting to input from our senses.

Another way to enhance focus is by harnessing **brainwave synchronization.** This phenomenon suggests that brainwaves naturally synchronize with external stimuli, like sound or flickering light.

You might wonder, "What the heck are brainwaves?" Scientifically known as neural oscillations, brainwaves are electrical impulses produced when neurons communicate. These waves occur at varying frequencies, some fast, some slow, and are measured in cycles per second, or hertz (Hz). The frequencies are known as gamma, beta, alpha, theta, and delta.

ALL ABOUT BRAINWAVES

GAMMA
(30–80 Hz)

Gamma waves, the fastest brainwaves, are associated with peak concentration, high-level information processing, perception and integrating sensory input into meaningful information.

BETA
(13–32 Hz)

Beta waves show up when we are awake, alert, and actively thinking. They are associated with focusing, problem solving, learning new concepts, and decision-making.

ALPHA
(8–13 Hz)

Alpha waves are produced when we are in states of physical and mental relaxation, like when meditating or before falling asleep. They are associated with creative imagination and subconscious activity.

THETA
(4–8 Hz)

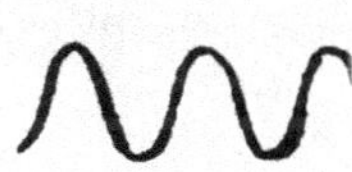

Theta waves can be present during daydreaming, deep hypnosis, and light sleep, such as right before we wake. Theta waves are associated with memory processing, creativity and intuition.

DELTA
(0.5–4 Hz)

Delta waves are the slowest and are produced when we are in a state of deep, dreamless sleep.

Brainwave synchronization is based on the premise that the brain is composed of millions of neurons interacting with each other through electrical signals that create brainwaves. When the brain experiences an external stimulus through any sensory organ, it responds with electrical activity called the **cortical evoked response (CER).** The CER is generated from periodic rhythmic stimuli in the form of sound or light frequencies.

A common and accessible way to take advantage of brainwave synchronization is with the use of binaural beats. When you listen to two tones, each with a different frequency and one in each ear (headphones required), the brain creates the perception of a third tone. This third tone is called a binaural beat and is heard at the frequency between the two tones.

When a binaural beat is sustained over time, it causes the CER to synchronize your brainwaves to the frequency of the beat. This synchronization can enhance brain function, depending on the frequency introduced.

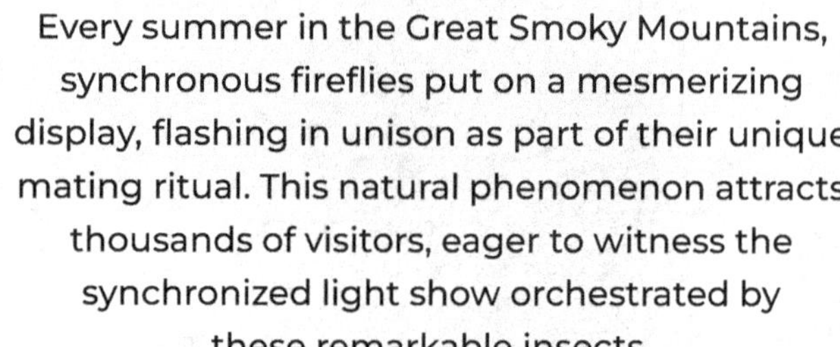

Every summer in the Great Smoky Mountains, synchronous fireflies put on a mesmerizing display, flashing in unison as part of their unique mating ritual. This natural phenomenon attracts thousands of visitors, eager to witness the synchronized light show orchestrated by these remarkable insects.

Everyone gets distracted. The real divide is between those who quickly get back on track and those who let interruptions expand into longer periods of inactivity. As attention spans get shorter, you can separate yourself from the crowd and achieve wild success simply by cultivating your ability to focus. A trained mind is more powerful than a heat-seeking missile and more useful than a smartphone.

Good advice: Pay no mind to the undesired aspects of life beyond the lessons they impart. Keep your focus on the path forward.

FOCUS TOOL:
MEDITATION AND BRAINWAVE SYNCHRONIZATION

**Here's a quick guide to get you
started with meditation:**

Sit in a comfortable upright position.

Close your eyes or rest them on a fixed spot or candle flame; bring your attention to the sound of your breathing. Follow the entire cycle of each breath attentively, noting the sound and sensation each time you inhale and exhale.

The mind will naturally wander, so don't beat yourself up when you notice this. Simply guide your attention back to your breathing.

Start with short periods. Even two minutes of a still mind can be transformational. Five minutes in the morning and five minutes at night is a great starting goal.

Experiment with adding a mantra to your practice. Your mantra can be any word or phrase you repeat with each cycle of breath. For example, "Peace."

Add binaural beats for your desired brainwave state as background audio for your meditation practice.

Meditation may be challenging at first. The more challenging it is, the more benefits it will likely impart to you. As you practice, give yourself grace to learn this new skill. Over time the rewards will become evident, improving your clarity, focus, and overall well-being.

Communication

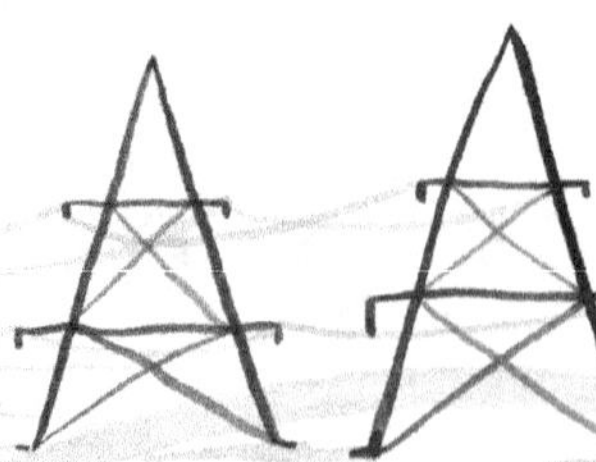

We've explored awareness and focus, so now we turn to our internal and external communication. This is where the most transformative shifts can occur.

Power lines and virtual lines of communication, like WiFi, energize everything in our environment, providing a stable connection that enriches our lives. As a social species, we need secure connections, both with ourselves and with the greater community. These connections are essential for our well-being, fostering a sense of belonging and support.

Changing how we speak to ourselves is at the core of training our minds. After all, our inner dialogue is with us at every moment of every day and we speak to ourselves more than anyone else.

In the absence of healthy and supportive communication with ourselves, our inner dialogue can be a curse leading to self-criticism, overthinking, worry, and anxiety. However, once we shift the narrative, the opposite is true. Our inner voice can become our loving guide, coach, and a source of creativity.

Many of us believe that our inner voice represents our true self; however, we often fail to recognize that this inner voice is a collection of stories and beliefs we've internalized from our families, education, and life experiences. These beliefs compose our self-identity or ego. By applying awareness to our thought patterns and reflecting on the environments in which we grew up, we begin to identify and release stories and false beliefs that do not serve us. These are limiting beliefs and they fuel negative self-talk.

Here are some examples of limiting beliefs:

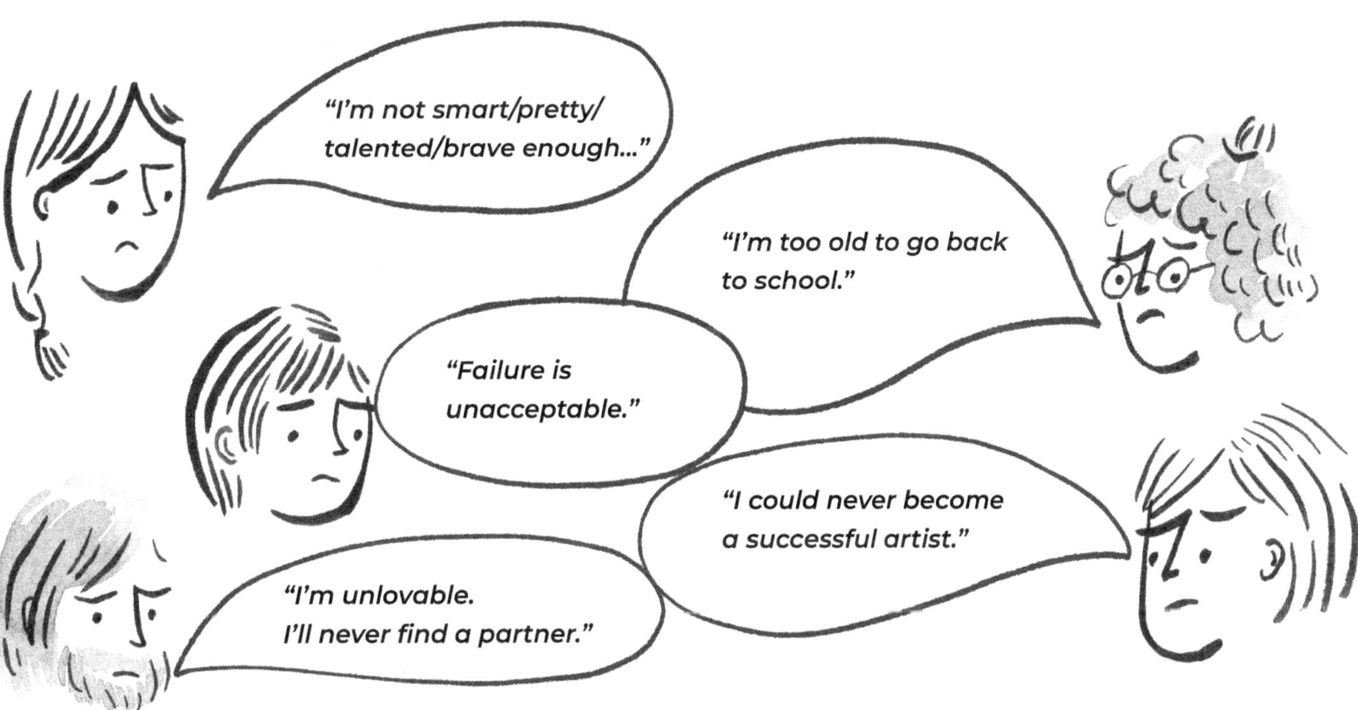

These beliefs imprison us in disempowering narratives that restrict us from living authentically and pursuing our true interests. If you look at your limiting beliefs critically, you'll also see they aren't based on any discernible truths.

As I pointed out earlier, the brain's plasticity allows it to change at any age. This means we all have the ability to learn new skills, overcome challenges, and improve our mental and physical well-being at any stage of our life. Everyone is dealt a different hand in life—some of us learn skills and positive self-belief at a young age, while others acquire these later in life. The timing of each journey is unique, and that is perfectly perfect.

Once we become aware of how we speak to ourselves and the words we use, we can begin to break the patterns. For example:

Simple changes in the language we use can shape how we see ourselves and our capabilities.

Paying attention to how we speak to ourselves when we make mistakes is another key to changing our internal communication. So often, we're our own worst critic, shaming ourselves when things go wrong.

Susan Kennedy, also known as SARK, brings a playful approach to the topic of self-talk. She uses the term "inner critics" to personify negative self-talk and teaches that these critics are formed early in our childhood to help us cope and survive. She assigns names like Procrastinator or Perfectionist to the inner critics that relate to their specific personality and criticisms, which usually revolve around the idea that we just aren't good enough. SARK explains that we do not prosper because we are bombarded by the relentless, harsh, critical, berating, and diminishing messages of these inner critics.[84]

In addition to giving the inner critics jobs to occupy them; like sending the Perfectionist to an egg factory to check each egg for cracked shells, SARK suggests an elegantly simple solution to deal with them—call upon the power of the word "actually." She recommends interrupting the inner critic's monologue with "actually," followed by a countering statement.

For example, if the inner critic says, "Things never work out for me," you can respond with, "Actually, I did very well at this just last week."

The other side of the communication coin is effective external communication. Our relationship with ourselves significantly impacts how we communicate with others. The clearer we see ourselves, the easier it becomes to understand other people's perspectives.

What we hear from others is filtered through our beliefs, past experiences, and emotional wounds. When we are triggered into emotional reactions, it indicates there is valuable information to be gleaned. **By adding self-awareness to our interactions, we can achieve relational awareness.**

Self-awareness is an internal journey, whereas relational awareness encompasses both internal and external components—recognizing that the other person's *truth* is shaped by their unique experiences.

With relational awareness, we get better at empathizing, communicating, and avoiding conflicts by appreciating one another's unique perspective. This helps build stronger, more meaningful relationships and boosts our personal growth and emotional intelligence.

For successful communication, it's best to clear up misunderstandings quickly and express our needs calmly. Staying calm and regulated is crucial. When we're emotional or stressed, we go into fight-or-flight mode, trying to defend our position or escape. This isn't the best time for clear, compassionate communication. Instead, we can take a break to allow our nervous system to calm down and then return to the conversation.

The philosopher Eugene Fordsworthe is credited with saying that assumption is the mother of all mistakes. We are often guilty of drawing conclusions without having all the information, and these assumptions are frequently wrong.

In interpersonal situations, assumptions are usually the result of poor communication. Instead of asking for clarification, we assume we understand someone's position or intent, leading to abundant misunderstandings.

We then obsess over these assumptions, overthinking and creating stories. Sometimes, all it takes is to ask for clarification to dissolve these assumptions. One rule to remember for effective communication is never to make assumptions. Our perspectives can be both different and true simultaneously.

We can learn to establish and clearly communicate boundaries to protect our energy and maintain healthy relationships.

Those who tend to sacrifice their own needs for others (hello people pleasers!) may struggle with setting healthy boundaries.

Identifying and effectively communicating your needs is a powerful way to practice self-love. It also helps us build fulfilling, mutually respectful relationships that fill our cups rather than deplete us.

COMMUNICATION TOOL: HYPNOSIS

Hypnosis is a powerful way to communicate with the subconscious mind. Often misunderstood, and misrepresented by Hollywood, hypnosis is perfectly safe. You cannot get stuck in an alternate universe, nor will you cluck like a chicken unless you specifically ask your hypnotist to assist you in that pursuit; after all, who am I to judge?

Recognized by the American Medical Association in 1958 as a valid and useful treatment, hypnosis is essentially focused, selective attention accompanied by heightened suggestibility. Increased suggestibility can occur for several reasons, including being in a heightened state of emotion or, conversely, being deeply relaxed.

The combination of selective attention and suggestibility allows us to communicate more effectively with our subconscious mind, enabling us to program and reprogram it. Whether we are conscious of it or not, we are always being programmed.

In a state of hypnosis, our critical analytical conscious mind takes a break, allowing new perspectives to emerge and increasing cognitive flexibility and flow.

Hypnosis has been used for centuries, dating back to ancient Egypt and Greece, where it was employed for healing purposes. Modern neuroscience has shown, that hypnosis can alter brain activity— enhancing creativity, reducing pain, and even improving immune function. Elite athletes and performers often use hypnosis to enhance focus, overcome mental barriers, and achieve peak performance.

Self-Hypnosis or Guided Hypnosis?

The difference between them lies in who facilitates the process.

Self-hypnosis is performed independently by the individual using relaxation, concentration, and suggestion techniques to enter a trance-like state.

Self-hypnosis enhances our control of the mind-body connection and provides a communication pathway to our deep mind.

Just as self-massage feels different from a therapist's massage, self-hypnosis feels different from being hypnotized by a practitioner. Both methods offer distinct benefits.

Guided hypnosis, is led by a trained hypnotist who guides the individual through the process to achieve the desired state and outcomes. Working with a skilled practitioner offers the added benefit of helping you identify blind spots and crafting language and potent suggestions that your mind can more easily absorb.

Age regression hypnosis is a technique that allows a hypnotherapist to guide a client back in time to address and resolve a client's current problems and concerns. Once a connection between the past and present is established, the hypnotized client is guided to uncover the initial sensitizing event from their past. The hypnotherapist then helps the client to resolve their misperceptions and misunderstandings. Emotions are often released, and new empowering perspectives are introduced, leading to healing.

You are invited to experience a complimentary taste of hypnosis at:
https://mindmoodvibe.com/mindmanualhypnosis

MIRACULOUS MIND POWER: DALE CARNEGIE[87]

AUTOSUGGESTION

CONTROLLED
ATTENTION

SELF-DISCIPLINE

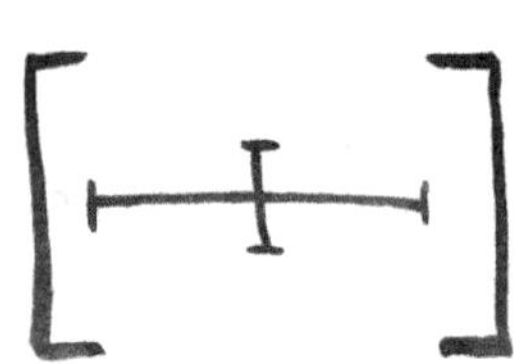

DEFINITENESS
OF PURPOSE

WILLPOWER—
ACTIVELY ENGAGED

Action

Lightning strikes with swift and decisive action, and when it connects with the ground, it magnetizes soil, rocks, and metals. Similarly, taking action engages our brain in problem-solving mode, magnetizing us to our tasks or goals. Just as lightning can transform the elements it touches, decisive action can transform our mindset and propel us toward success.

Contrary to popular myth, lightning can strike in the same place twice.

Venezuela hosts the world's most active lightning hotspot. Nocturnal thunderstorms take place over Lake Maracaibo in the northwest of the country on average 297 days of the year. These thunderstorms produce a whopping 232 lightning strikes per square kilometer each year.

When speaking of action, it's important to distinguish between effective, purposeful, strategic action and busy work.

When faced with a deadline or a daunting to-do list, many of us might clean our house or organize our email inbox instead. Although these behaviors technically qualify as action, they are better classified as effortful distractions. James Clear refers to this type of action as "motion."

By choosing to take strategic baby steps aligned with our true goals, we move in the right direction rather than in circles. You may ask, "If motion doesn't lead to results, why do we do it?" The answer is that, more often than not, we engage in motion because it allows us to feel like we're making progress without the risk of failure.[88]

Motion is indeed movement, but targeted action is what truly moves the needle forward. For instance, if your goal is to run a marathon, spending hours on Google to look for local trainers and reading every available review is motion; putting on your running shoes and going for a run is action.

Taking action can be challenging because it requires breaking free from programmed habits. By design, our minds seek homeostasis and favor the path of least resistance. The comfort zone feels safe and familiar, making change difficult. However, understanding how the mind works and using clever tools and techniques can make taking action easier.

Habits are the building blocks of our daily lives, but many operate beyond our conscious awareness. We often overlook them while focusing on what we deem more important. By paying attention to our habits, we gain the power to evaluate which ones to keep, upgrade, or replace. Habits form because the brain prefers patterns that reduce cognitive load and provide a sense of safety, which is why they can be so hard to change.

In his book, *The Power of Focus,* Jack Canfield begins with a quote from American educationist Horace Mann: "A habit is a cable we weave, a thread each day, and at last, we cannot break it."[90] But with the right tools, we can trick our brains into being more flexible and open to change.

Starting small with habits is essential for making them enduring practices. Begin by committing to a new habit for just two minutes each day. Often, the most challenging part is getting started, but a small commitment can unexpectedly extend beyond the initial timeframe. These small steps accumulate, building momentum and facilitating lasting change.

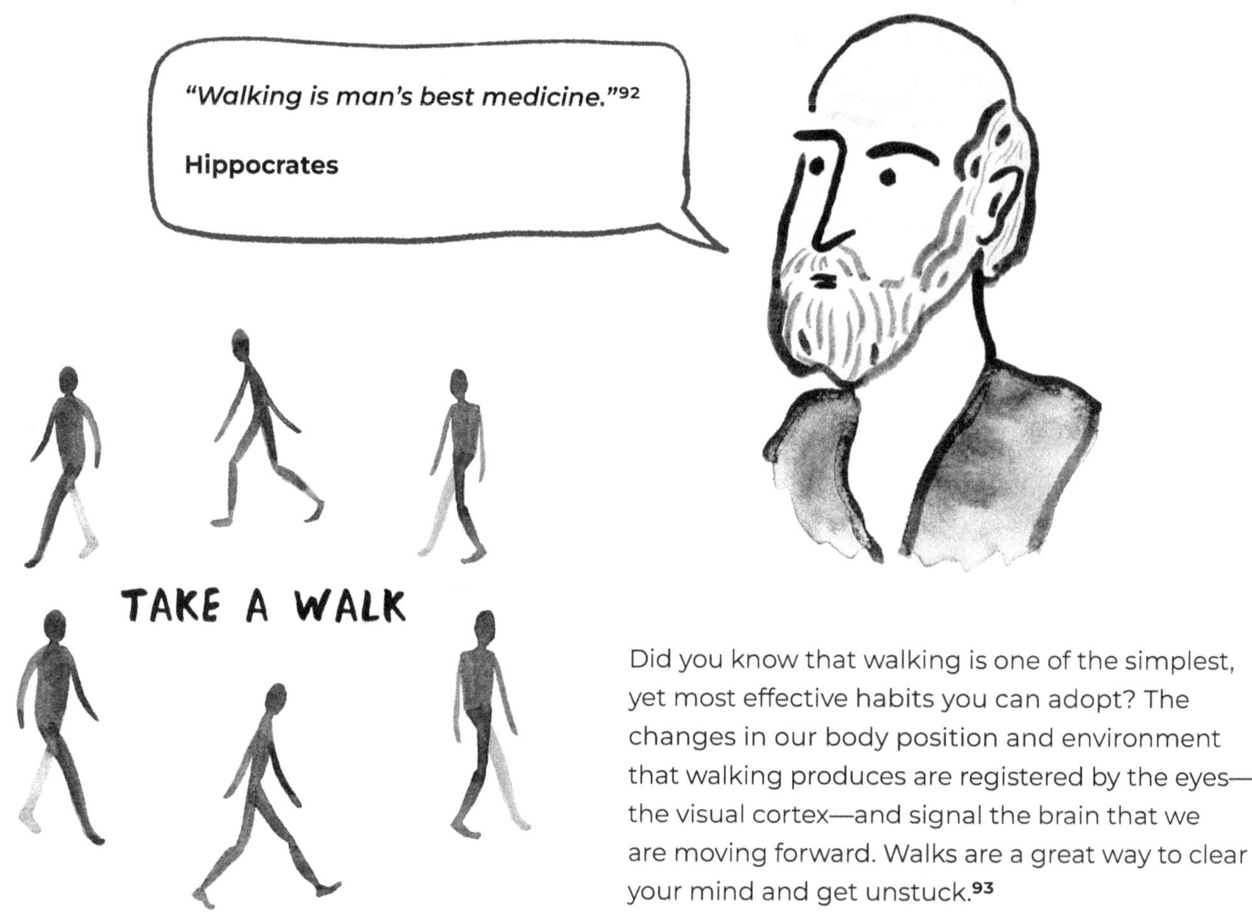

Did you know that walking is one of the simplest, yet most effective habits you can adopt? The changes in our body position and environment that walking produces are registered by the eyes—the visual cortex—and signal the brain that we are moving forward. Walks are a great way to clear your mind and get unstuck.[93]

Note: One can be easily overwhelmed by the sheer number of habits that could potentially be incorporated into your routine. A practical analogy is when choosing supplements to improve health. Forty different supplements may on some level be beneficial for your health, but taken together on a daily basis will probably put your liver and kidneys in distress.

At some point, adding more habits may reach a point of diminishing return. We are aiming for balanced ease, not disciplined perfection. When tackling new habits, look for those that benefit more than one dimension of wellness: mental, emotional, physical, spiritual, social, financial, etc. Make sure your habit plan is balanced; if you are completely stressed out by your habits, they probably need a redesign.

ACTION TOOL:

How to build great habits:

Create habits based on your desired identity, rather than on an obligatory to-do list. The subconscious mind works well with vivid and emotional mental pictures and "I am" statements like "I am fit and in the best shape of my life" rather than task lists like "I will work out for three hours every day."

Answer the question "why?" Getting in touch with the reason you want to create a new habit is the first step in building a habit that lasts. A sense of purpose makes taking action much easier.

Set small goals based on a bigger vision. When our subconscious mind sees the desired result, it has a blueprint to follow. These incremental steps make the larger vision more manageable and achievable, allowing us to build confidence and maintain motivation as we progress.

Stack habits. Combine established habits with new ones to link them together. This could look like "When I brush my teeth, I will reflect on three things I'm grateful for" or, "While I'm waiting for my coffee to brew in the morning, I will meditate for two minutes." Stacking habits is a great way to maximize results in a short time.

Make habits fun! Exercise by playing a sport instead of forcing yourself to run five miles three times a week. Take a daily walk while listening to your favorite feel-good playlist or by calling someone you love.

How to Fortify Your Mind

Now that we have a clear understanding of how the mind works, we know that much of its function is automatic and unconscious. In our information-saturated world, it's impossible to fully evaluate or verify every piece of information we encounter. Our minds naturally seek shortcuts and the path of least resistance to conserve energy and reduce cognitive load. While these preferences help prevent overload, they also make us vulnerable to manipulation by those who know how to exploit these mental shortcuts.

This is the primary goal of advertisements, propaganda, political agendas, social media platforms, and smartphone apps. To defend our mental fortress and free ourselves from mind control, we first need an awareness of how we are influenced. By pointing out the penetrable aspects of our psychology, we can fortify our minds against unwanted influence. **We decide whether we are going to be the programmers or the ones being programmed.**

Billions of dollars have been spent to figure out the secrets of how to manipulate the mind, and it turns out that there is a science to why we say "yes."

In his book *Influence*, Robert Cialdini outlines six "levers of influence" that exploit our psychology and make us more likely to agree to a proposition.[96]

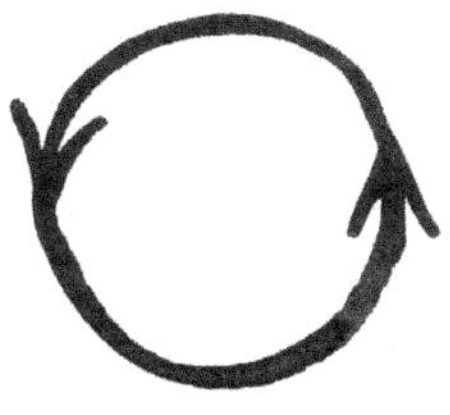

RECIPROCATION

COMMITMENT & CONSISTENCY

SOCIAL PROOF

LIKING

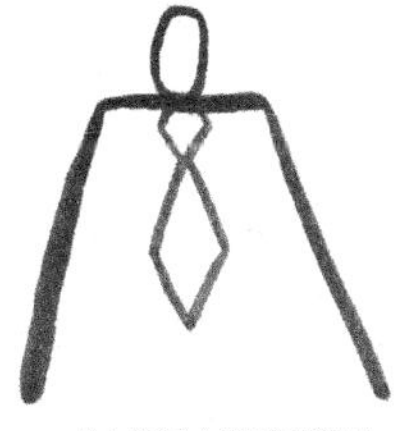

AUTHORITY

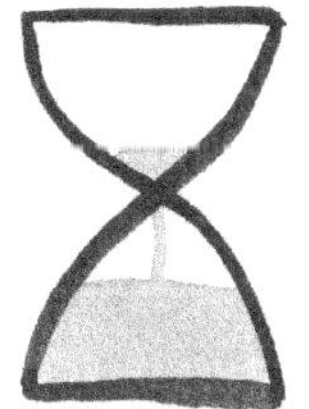

SCARCITY

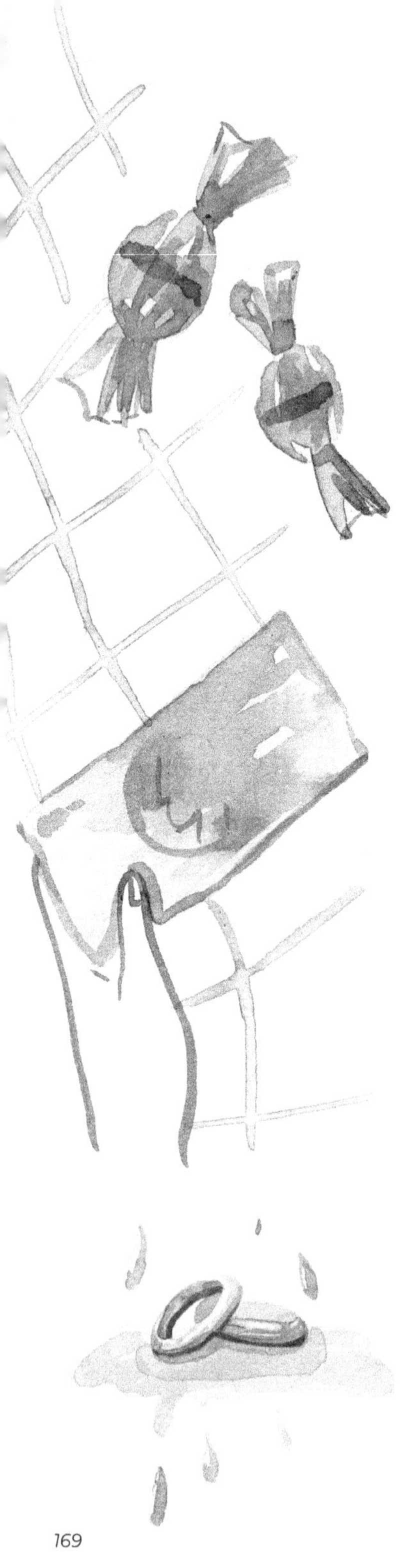

Reciprocation

This lever is predicated on the feeling of indebtedness that causes us to feel that we have to repay what someone has given us or done for us. The strong urge to reciprocate favors and gifts stems from our evolution as a social species. Strong social cohesion and the ability to work together gave our ancestors, and continue to give us today, a better chance at survival. That is why repaying an act of kindness feels like common decency.

Some examples of this principle in action:

* Free samples at a grocery store to urge you to buy a product you might not have considered otherwise.
* Someone buying you dinner on a date or a drink at the bar to persuade you to spend time with them.
* A server bringing complimentary after-dinner mints with your bill. Studies show that this increases the likelihood of receiving a larger tip.

Commitment & Consistency

This lever is based on our strong desire to be, and appear to be, consistent with what we already did, said, or decided. In fact, we will convince ourselves that our current actions or beliefs align with past ones, even when they clearly do not.

Examples of this principle are:

* Gamblers who are unsure of their bets before they are placed but become far more confident after they are set. They will often claim afterward that they were always confident in that bet.
* People who stay in a marriage even when divorce is the best option, to maintain their commitment to the promise "til death do us part." This often involves a desire to appear consistent to one's family, or community to avoid judgment.
* People who publicly announce a decision to their friend group or community, which motivates them to follow through.

Social Proof

The essence of this lever is that we decide what is correct based on what the majority of other people think is correct. The idea is that if many people act in a specific way, it must be worthy of imitation.

Some examples of this principle:

* A crowd of people gawking at something in the street makes us join the gawkers to see what the commotion is about.
* Laughing at a joke when everyone else laughs, even though you really didn't get the punchline.
* All sorts of trends including fashion, social media, and technology gain popularity as the influential join in.

Liking

This lever suggests that we are more likely to comply with requests from people we know and like, stemming from our evolutionary past built around tight-knit social groups. This principle is heavily influenced by how physically attractive someone is and how similar to us we perceive them to be. Receiving compliments also increases our liking of others.

Real-world examples include:

* Celebrity endorsement of products that boost sales dramatically.
* Compliments from friendly attractive salespeople that build trust and warm customers up to their product recommendations.
* A willingness to lend money to a friend, which you would not extend to a stranger on the street.

Authority

In most cultures, children are taught to obey authority. This lever of influence on our behavior is based on the sociocultural tendency to comply with requests from acknowledged sources of authority, such as police officers, teachers, doctors, and judges, to name just a few. Appearance plays a significant role in this principle, as we often recognize authority through uniforms, badges, and formal clothing. Con artists frequently take advantage of this principle because it is relatively easy to appear as an authority figure.

Some examples of this principle at work:

* We are more willing to move our vehicle if a police officer asks than if the request comes from another driver.
* We have more respect for people with titles, such as Ph.D., doctor, or president.
* Willingness to follow medical advice from a "doctor on television" who is not actually an MD in real life.

Scarcity

The scarcity lever acts upon the human tendency to view opportunities or products as more valuable when their availability is limited. Psychologically we think that if something is scarce, it must be in high demand, which means that it is something of quality or desire. This principle relates to Prospect Theory, also known as loss aversion, which states that the fear of loss tends to outweigh the desire for gain.

We see examples of this principle in the following:

- Limited-time offers.
- Deadlines (Black Friday, Cyber Monday).
- "First come, first served."
- Exclusive, limited-quantity items.

"If you aren't paying for the product, you are the product."[99]

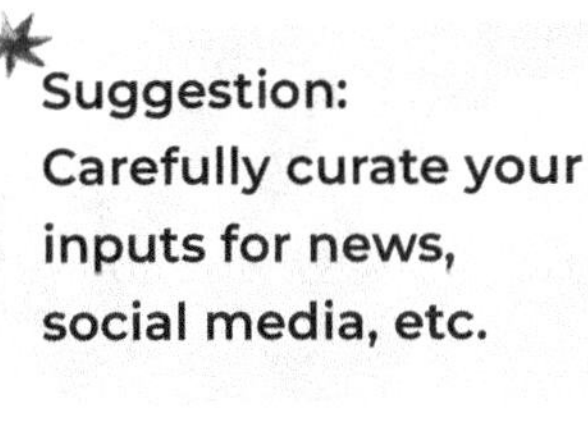

**Suggestion:
Carefully curate your inputs for news, social media, etc.**

While these different levers are not always employed to nefarious ends, (maybe you just want to enjoy the free samples at Costco without feeling manipulated into purchasing something. That's important, too!) being aware of the techniques people use to persuade us of something can help protect us. There can be danger in blind obedience. One example is a nurse who fails to question obvious medical errors made by physicians in positions of authority.

Across history, genocides and mass atrocities have not been carried out by a few isolated individuals alone, but sustained by the quiet compliance—or silence—of many ordinary people trying to preserve normalcy or avoid personal risk.

Cognitive overload significantly influences what we believe or buy. In a fast-paced life, our decision-making narrows, especially when we are stressed, uncertain, rushed, or tired. Under these circumstances, we often rely on just one piece of evidence. Decision-making is challenged further when we cannot trust our sources. The struggle is indeed real.

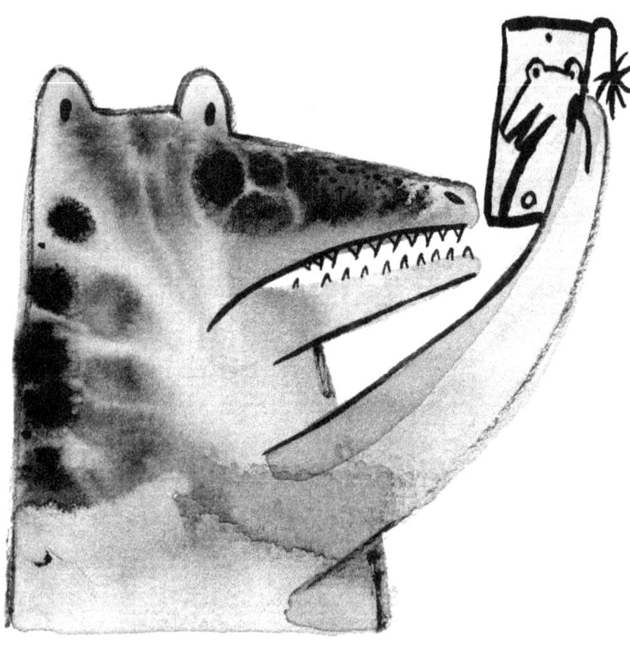

Another pillar of a fortified mind is accurate thinking. Accurate thinking involves separating fact from fiction and opinions, and separating important facts from unimportant ones. Important facts are those that aid in the attainment of your goals and purpose. Unimportant facts include the fact that crocodiles cannot stick out their tongues.

Accurate thinking can be strengthened with logic and rational thought. Simply put, logic is the study of correct reasoning. Correct reasoning, or critical thinking, allows us to come to accurate conclusions about the world around us without being deluded by our senses, emotions, or memory. Critical thinking entails effective communication, problem-solving, and a commitment to overcome our innate egocentrism, which means seeing things from perspectives other than our own.

As we saw in the section on communication, our minds have the tendency to make assumptions and jump to conclusions when we don't have all the information. This is harmful because we base our beliefs and actions on flawed information, which inevitably creates unnecessary stress and drama.

Training our minds to think rationally is essential if we want to change our minds. It helps us move through life with ease and grace.

Learning about logical fallacies is one way to work on our critical thinking skills. A logical fallacy is a flaw in reasoning that is like a trick of thought. They are often deviously employed by politicians and the media to sway our opinion.

When considering a source or opinion, ask:

What's the possible motive?

Is there profit or personal interest?

Can the information be verified?

What is the writer's reputation?

Is the information overzealous or sensational?

Be wary of accepting anything as fact that arises from senses, emotions, or memory.

A logical fallacy observed frequently in politics is the **strawman fallacy:**
Misrepresenting someone's argument or position to make it easier to attack.
A reasonable idea is inflated into an extreme one—then rejected for being unreasonable.
For example, one person says, "I think we should spend less time on our phones."
Another responds, "So you want everyone to abandon technology and live like it's the 1800s?"

PROPAGANDA MODEL OF MEDIA

In *Manufacturing Consent,*[100] Noam Chomsky and Edward Herman outline **five filters that shape how we receive information.**

1. **Ownership:** The media works as propaganda machines for the corporations that pay them.

2. **Advertising:** Advertisers want consumers to fall in line with the interests of the company they are trying to produce results for. Information is released with an eye on the bottom line instead of whether it is true or helpful.

3. **Establishment:** Governments and corporations know how to influence the narrative. They supply the stories and interviews that control public perception. Any challenges to power are labeled as fringe opinions from the far left or far right.

4. **Flak:** When a story is inconvenient, those in power will try to discredit the messengers.

5. **Fear:** Instilling fear of a common enemy, whether disease, minorities etc; strengthens public consensus and makes the story more difficult to challenge.

Spend some time investigating the various logical fallacies to gain an understanding of the ways in which we come to incorrect conclusions.

Psychological operations—US Government funded programs that were declassified:

- PROJECT ARTICHOKE
- PROJECT BLUEBIRD
- PROJECT CHATTER
- PROJECT MK DELTA
- PROJECT MK NAOMI
- PROJECT MK ULTRA
- PROJECT STARGATE

The CIA's mind control program known as MKUltra was a 10-year program implemented to find ways by which to control and exploit human behavior. Drugs like LSD and mescaline were used in experiments to see if their effects could be leveraged as tools to interrogate and control the mind. In fact, in the early 1950s, Sidney Gottlieb, the chief chemist of the CIA, organized the organization's purchase of the entire world's supply of LSD,[101] which he had shipped to the United States. The irony here is that the CIA then unwittingly became the instigator of the LSD counterculture. Everyone in the US who took LSD, from Alan Ginsberg to the Grateful Dead, got it from the CIA.[102]

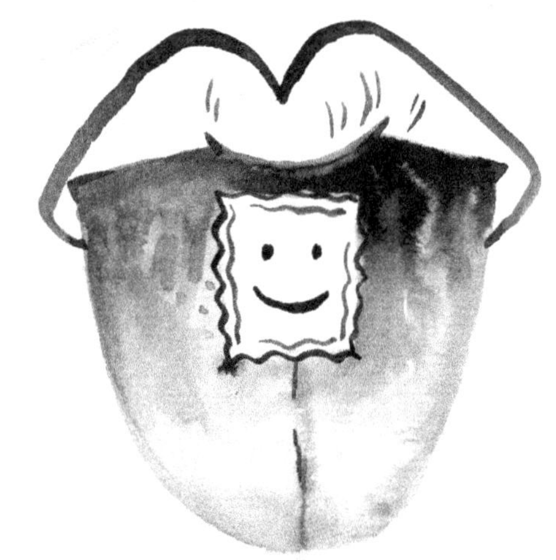

Conclusion

Congratulations on reaching the end of the *Mind Manual!*

What a journey it has been. One of exploration, growth, and insight into the miraculous capabilities of your mind.

Along the way, you've discovered not only the structure of the mind but also the subtle forces, like vibration, that shape your reality. By learning to raise your mental frequency, you now hold the power to elevate your life experiences.

We've covered the hardware and software of the mind, explored the conscious and subconscious, and recognized the deep interconnection between mind and body. You've learned practical tools for improving attention, fostering curiosity, and developing self-compassion. But most importantly, you've seen how becoming aware of your mind's patterns can free you from fear and resistance, helping you shed limiting beliefs that no longer serve you.

The true power of this book lies not just in the knowledge you've gained, but in the vibration you now embody. By beginning to train your mind, you've unlocked the potential to guide your life toward more joy, connection, and fulfillment. This is not the end of your journey, but the beginning of a life filled with elevated vibes and limitless possibilities.

So don't stop here. Keep reading, keep learning, and keep growing. Countless resources are available to help you continue your education. For practical yet innovative applications of the principles presented in this book, head over to **www.mindmoodvibe.com.**

Remember, the more you align with your authentic self, the more magic you infuse into your world. So keep learning, keep evolving, and continue to raise your vibe. The power to transform your life is, and always will be, within your beautiful mind.

The Seven Hermetic Principles and the Mind

These principles synthesize ancient teachings with modern scientific and metaphysical concepts. They reveal the inner workings of consciousness, thought, and emotion, offering us a deeper understanding of how the mind mirrors universal laws. By applying these timeless truths, we can raise our mental vibration, harmonize opposing forces within us, and align our inner world with the greater patterns of reality.

✳ 1. The Principle of Mentalism

The mind is the architect of reality. As ancient Hermetic teachings suggest, everything is mental in origin. Today, quantum physics affirms that consciousness shapes the world around us. Our thoughts, beliefs, and perceptions create the very fabric of our experience. In the realm of the mind, possibilities unfold as we realize that reality begins in the mental plane, allowing us to craft a life aligned with our highest potential.

✳ 2. The Principle of Correspondence

"As above, so below." The patterns of the universe are echoed within us. From the fractal geometry in nature to the holographic nature of the cosmos, the mind reflects the same organization. Just as the macrocosm and microcosm mirror each other, the workings of our inner mind correspond to the world we create externally. By understanding these patterns, we can elevate our mind and synchronize with the vast rhythms around us.

✳ 3. The Principle of Vibration

All thoughts, emotions, and mental states vibrate at their own frequencies. Just as atoms are swirling vortices of energy, the mind operates through vibrations that ripple into the world around us. When we raise our mental and emotional frequencies, we tune into higher realms of experience, attracting greater clarity, peace, and creativity. The mind, like the universe, is in constant motion, and we are free to choose our frequency.

✳ 4. The Principle of Polarity

Opposites are merely different extremes of the same essence. What seems like a conflict (fear versus confidence, doubt versus belief) is simply a different position along one spectrum. By understanding this, we can transcend rigid thinking and find peace and balance in our thinking. When we embrace the truth of polarity, we are free to embrace all that life provides.

✳ 5. The Principle of Rhythm

The ebb and flow of thoughts and emotions follow a natural rhythm, much like the waves in the ocean. Just as the universe moves in cycles, so too does the mind. Periods of high inspiration are followed by moments of rest and reflection. Harmony is found in embracing the ups and downs of mental states, knowing that rhythm is not an obstacle but a guide toward equilibrium. By moving with the natural rhythm of thought, we optimize our life experience.

✳ 6. The Principle of Cause and Effect

Every mental state has an impact—no matter how seemingly insignificant. Every thought or emotion is linked in a chain of cause and effect that's often hidden away in our subconscious. By mastering the mind, we become the cause, rather than the effect, of our experiences. Mindful thoughts lead to mindful actions, creating a ripple that shapes our reality. Understanding this principle empowers us to take responsibility for the reality we manifest.

✳ 7. The Principle of Gender

The mind contains both masculine and feminine energies, each contributing their gifts. The masculine energy of the mind inspires structure, logic, and action, while the feminine energy fosters intuition, creativity, and growth. Together, these energies create a balanced mental state where logic and intuition coexist. By harmonizing these energies, we can nurture both action and reflection, creating from a place of power and balance.

Rules of Mind

Adapted and used with permission from the International Association of Counselors and Therapists.

 **The Mind and Body Are Inextricably Connected**

A change on one level (mentally, emotionally, or physically) equals a change on all other levels of being. Every thought sparks a reaction on both emotional and physical levels. Whether it manifests as a racing heart or a pit in your stomach, your thoughts trigger emotions that have tangible effects on your body. By training your mind to remain calm, you can master your health and happiness.

"Every change in the physiological state is accompanied by an appropriate change in the mental emotional state, conscious or unconscious, and conversely every change in the mental emotional state, conscious or unconscious, is accompanied by an appropriate change in the physiological state."[103]

Elmer Green

 **What Is Expected Tends to Be Realized**

Repeated exposure to the same mental image will create a blueprint that your subconscious mind begins to manifest. This is how expectations can become self-fulfilling prophecies, for better or worse. And the reason is that the same parts of your brain are activated whether you are really experiencing something or just observing and imagining it.

 **Emotion Is More Powerful Than Reason or Willpower**

Think about how much easier it was to get out of bed on Christmas morning compared to exam day when you were younger. Any idea accompanied by strong emotion is tough to overcome with reason alone. Emotion is more powerful than reason or willpower. This is because emotions create a sense of urgency and importance, driving us to act immediately, while reasoned decisions often require more deliberate thought and consideration. Emotional responses are deeply ingrained in our survival mechanisms, making them more instinctive and influential on our behavior.

 ### 4 Imagination and Memory Are Easily Confused

If you imagine something with enough detail and conviction, your subconscious mind begins to operate as if it truly happened. This can be a double-edged sword. Imagining traumatic events can cause powerful biochemicals to flow in your body, causing harm. Conversely any healing you experience, whether based on real or imagined events, persists. This highlights the powerful influence of the mind on both our psychological and physical states.

 ### 5 An Idea Accepted by the Subconscious Mind Will Remain Until it Is Replaced

Once your subconscious mind accepts an idea, that idea tends to stick. The longer it stays, the stronger the habit or belief becomes. Awareness is the key to ungluing ideas that do not serve your best interest. Recognize these ingrained beliefs, challenge them, and watch your life transform as you break free from old patterns and embrace new, empowering possibilities.

 ### 6 You Are Either a Programmer or You Are One of the Programmed

Your mind constantly sifts through perceived information to create meaning. External sources, like advertising and media, also deliver meaning. As a programmer of your mind, you consciously sort for empowering messages and question those that are disempowering or fear-based. If you remain one of the programmed, you are simply tossed about in the chaos, adopting or resisting the pre-programmed meanings presented to you. Embrace your role as the programmer to navigate through the noise and shape your reality.

 ### 7 When Dealing with the Subconscious Mind, the Greater the Conscious Effort, the Less the Subconscious Response

Imagine a set of scales tipping back and forth: when the conscious mind is active, the subconscious mind is less so, and vice versa. Trying too hard creates resistance, often leading to self-defeat by producing the opposite of what is desired. Using mental force presupposes opposition, but the act of imagining opposition creates it. When your attention is focused on obstacles, you are not focused on the goal. To achieve success, relax your conscious effort and allow the subconscious mind to work without interference.

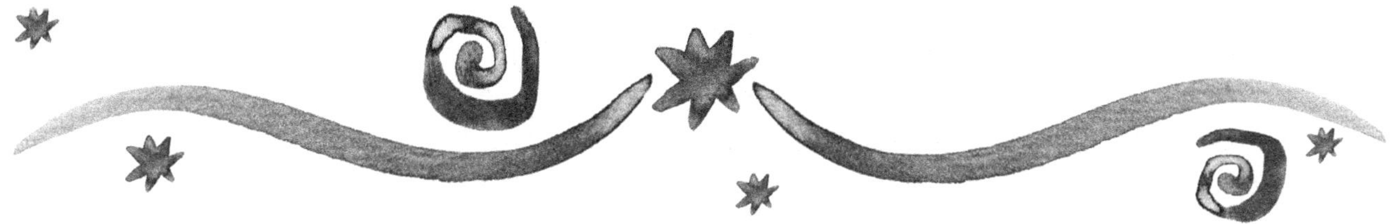

Bibliography

Ahmed, Waqās. "The Mind of Leonardo da Vinci." *Philosophy Now* 134, 2019.
https://philosophynow.org/issues/134/The_Mind_of_Leonardo_da_Vinci.

Ampel, Benjamin C., Mark Muraven, and Ewan C. McNay. "Mental Work Requires Physical Energy:
Self-Control Is Neither Exception nor Exceptional." *Frontiers in Psychology* 9, article 1005 (2018).
https://doi.org/10.3389/fpsyg.2018.01005.

Bandler, Richard, and John Grinder. *The Structure of Magic, Vol. 1: A Book About Language and Therapy.*
Palo Alto: Science and Behavior Books, 2005.

Batman, David C. "Hippocrates: Walking is Man's Best Medicine!" *Occupational Medicine* 62,
no. 5 (2012): 320–322. https://doi.org/10.1093/occmed/kqs084.

Beckett, Max. "History of the Internet: A Timeline Throughout the Years." July 6, 2023.
https://www.uswitch.com/broadband/guides/broadband-history/.

Blake, William. *The Marriage of Heaven and Hell.* 1790.
https://www.gutenberg.org/files/45315/45315-h/45315-h.htm.

Bradley, Marion Zimmer. *The Mists of Avalon.* New York: Ballantine Books, 1982.

Briggs, Lyndall, and Gary Green. *Soul Purpose: Self Development Stories, Quotes and Poems.*
Kingsgrove, NSW: SelfDevelopment.biz, 2003.

Buzsáki, György. *The Brain from Inside Out.* New York: Oxford University Press, 2018.

Campbell, Joseph, and Bill Moyers. *The Power of Myth: Programs 1-6.* Narrated by the authors.
Houston: High Bridge, 2007.

Canfield, Jack, Mark Victor Hansen, and Les Hewitt. *The Power of Focus* (revised edition).
New York: Random House, 2013.

Chaudon, Louis Mayeul. *Historical and Critical Memoirs of the Life and Writings of M. De Voltaire.*
London: G. G. J. and J. Robinson, 1786.

Chillot, Rick. "The Power of Touch." *Psychology Today*, March 11, 2013.
https://www.psychologytoday.com/articles/the-power-of-touch.

Chomsky, Noam. "The 5 Filters of the Mass Media Machine."
YouTube video, March 2, 2017. https://www.youtube.com/watch?v=34LGPIXvU5M.

Chopra, Deepak. *Metahuman: Unleashing Your Infinite Potential.* Narrated by the author.
New York: Random House Audio, 2019.

Chopra, Deepak. *The Ultimate Deepak Chopra Collection*. Narrated by the author. Glenview, IL: Nightingale-Conant, 2014.

Churchill, Winston. *Onwards to Victory: War Speeches*. Compiled by Charles Eade. London: Cassell and Co., 1943. Speech delivered at Harvard University, September 6, 1943. https://www.harvardmagazine.com/2018/09/churchill-harvard-september-6-1943.

Cialdini, Robert B. *Influence: The Psychology of Persuasion* (rev. ed.). New York: Harper Business, 2006.

Clear, James. "3-2-1: Consistency, Anger, and Shaping the World." November 24, 2022. https://jamesclear.com/3-2-1/november-24-2022.

Clear, James. *Atomic Habits: An Easy and Proven Way to Build Good Habits and Break Bad Ones*. New York: Penguin Random House, 2022.

Clear, James. "The Mistake Smart People Make: Being In Motion vs. Taking Action." 2020. https://jamesclear.com/taking-action.

Colier, Nancy. "Negative Thinking: A Dangerous Addiction." *Psychology Today*, April 15, 2019. https://www.psychologytoday.com/za/blog/inviting-monkey-tea/201904/negative-thinking-dangerous-addiction.

Covey, Stephen R. *The 7 Habits of Highly Effective People: Powerful Lessons in Personal Change*. Narrated by the author. New York: Simon & Schuster Audio, 2003.

Cytowic, Richard E., and David M. Eagleman. *Wednesday is Indigo Blue: Discovering the Brain of Synesthesia*. Cambridge: Massachusetts Institute of Technology, 2009.

de Bruijn, Maaike J., and Michael Bender. "Olfactory Cues Are More Effective Than Visual Cues in Experimentally Triggering Autobiographical Memories." *Memory* 26, no. 4, 2018. https://doi.org/10.1080/09658211.2017.1381744.

De Spinoza, Benedict. *The Chief Works of Benedict de Spinoza*. Translated from Latin, with an introduction by R.H.M. Elwes, 1901. https://oll.libertyfund.org/title/elwes-the-chief-works-of-benedict-de-spinoza-vol-2.

De Spinoza, Benedict. *Ethics*, Part V: Of the Power of the Understanding, or of Human Freedom, Proposition III. https://www.gutenberg.org/files/3800/3800-h/3800-h.htm.

Descartes, Rene. *Discourse on Method*. 1637. https://brians.wsu.edu/2016/11/04/rene-descartes-discourse-on-method-1637/.

DeVor, Meadow. *The Worthy Mind: Transform Your Mindset. Strengthen Self-Worth*. Kindle Edition. Naperville, ILL: Sourcebooks, 2023.

Dhammananda, K. Sri. *How to Live Without Fear and Worry*. Malaysia, Buddhist Missionary Society, 1989.

The Dhammapada. Translated from Pāli by F. Max Müller. London: Curzon Press, 1870. Reprint, Abingdon-on-Thames, Oxfordshire: Routledge, 2013.

Dispenza, Joe. *Evolve Your Brain: The Science of Changing Your Mind*. Narrated by Sean Runnette. Old Saybrook, CT: Tantor Audio, 2017.

Dispenza, Joe. *You Are the Placebo: Making Your Mind Matter*. Carlsbad, CA: Hay House, 2014.

Dostoevsky, Fyodor. *The Possessed*. 1916. Translated by Constance Garnett. Project Gutenberg, 2005. https://www.gutenberg.org/files/8117/8117-h/8117-h.htm.

Dumont, Theron Q. *The Power of Concentration*. Narrated by Richard Powers. Ashland, OR: Blackstone Audio, 2018.

Einstein, Albert. *Essays in Science*. 1934. Translated by Alan Harris. Mineola, NY: Dover Publications, 2009.

Elman, Dave. *Hypnotherapy*. Portland, OR: Westwood Publishing Company, 1970.

Emerson, Ralph Waldo. "Self-Reliance." *Essays: First Series*. 1841. https://archive.vcu.edu/english/engweb/transcendentalism/authors/emerson/essays/.

Emerson, Ralph Waldo. "Montaigne; or, the Skeptic." *Representative Men*, 1850. https://quod.lib.umich.edu/e/emerson/4957107.0004.001/1:8?rgn=div1;view=fulltext.

Field, Tiffany. *Touch*. 2nd ed. Cambridge: MIT Press, 2014.

Fisher, Jeffrey D., Marvin Rytting and Richard Heslin. "Hands Touching Hands: Affective and Evaluative Effects of an Interpersonal Touch." *Sociometry* 39, no. 4 (1976): 416–421. https://doi.org/10.2307/3033506.

Freud, Sigmund. *The Interpretation of Dreams* (Die Traumdeutung). 1899.

Freud, Sigmund. *The Psychopathology of Everyday Life*. 1901. Translated by A. A. Brill. London: Macmillan, 1915.

Gallo, Carmine. "The Maya Angelou Quote That Will Radically Improve Your Business." *Forbes*, May 31, 2014. https://www.forbes.com/sites/carminegallo/2014/05/31/the-maya-angelou-quote-that-will-radically-improve-your-business/.

Gelb, Michael J. *How to Think Like Leonardo Da Vinci*. New York: Random House, 2004.

Glachet, Ophélie, and Mohamad El Haj. "Odor Is More Effective Than a Visual Cue or a Verbal Cue for The Recovery of Autobiographical Memories in AD." *Journal of Clinical and Experimental Neuropsychology* 43, no. 2, 2021: 129–143. https://doi.org/10.1080/13803395.2021.1882392.

Goodall, Jane. *Harvest for Hope*. New York: Hachette Book Group, 2005.

Goleman, Daniel. *Focus: The Hidden Driver of Excellence*. New York: HarperCollins, 2013.

Goldman, Lawrence. *Victorians and Numbers: Statistics and Society in Nineteenth Century Britain*. New York: Oxford University Press, 2009.

Green, Elmer. "Beyond Psychophysics." *Subtle Energies & Energy Medicine* 10, no. 1, 1999: 359–395. https://journals.sfu.ca/seemj/index.php/seemj/article/view/290.

Gross, Philip. "The Same River: Thirteen Variations on Heraclitus." *New Writing* 10, no. 3 (2013): 312-322. https://doi.org/10.1080/14790726.2013.804844.

Gyatso, Tenzin, Fourteenth Dalai Lama. *The Wheel of Life: Buddhist Perspectives on Cause and Effect* (rev. ed.). Translation by Jeffrey Hopkins of lectures given in London, 1984. Somerville, MA: Wisdom Publications, 2015.

Hall, Manly P. *The Secret Teachings of all Ages*. Illustrated by J. Augustus Knapp. South Orange, NJ: A & D Books, 2009.

Hawkins, David R. *Power vs. Force: The Hidden Determinants of Human Behavior*. Dublin, Ireland: Veritas, 2013.

Hill, Napoleon, and Don Green. *How to Own Your Own Mind*. Narrated by Robertson Dean. Ashland, OR: Blackstone Audio, 2017.

Hill, Napoleon. *How to Own Your Own Mind*. New York: TarcherPerigee, 2017.

Hirayama, Ryuji et al. "High-Speed Acoustic Holography with Arbitrary Scattering Objects." *Science Advances* 8, no. 24, 2022. https://doi.org/10.1126/sciadv.abn7614.

Horowitz, Alexandra. *Being a Dog: Following the Dog Into a World of Smell*. New York: Scribner, 2016.

Huberman, Andrew, and Joe Dispenza. "Feeling Stuck?" *Reprogram Yourself*, YouTube video, May 1, 2023. https://www.youtube.com/watch?v=CjQo7DebOgs.

Inzlicht, Michael, Elliot Berkman, and Nathaniel Elkins-Brown. "The Neuroscience of 'Ego Depletion' or: How the Brain Can Help Us Understand Why Self-Control Seems Limited." In *Social Neuroscience: Biological Approaches to Social Psychology*, edited by Eddie Harmon-Jones and Michael Inzlicht, 101-123. New York: Taylor & Francis, 2016.

Ja, Amishi P. *Peak Mind: Find Your Focus, Own Your Attention, Invest 12 Minutes a Day*. Narrated by Xe Sands. New York: Harper Audio, 2021.

James, William. "Is Life Worth Living?" *International Journal of Ethics* 6, no. 1, 1895. https://www.jstor.org/stable/2375619.

James, William. *Pragmatism: A New Name for Some Old Ways of Thinking*. London: Longmans, Green, and Company, 1909.

James, William. *The Varieties of Religious Experience*. 1902. Landenberg, PA: Delphi Classics, 2018.

Johnson, Samuel. Preface to *A Dictionary of the English Language*. 1755.
https://johnsonsdictionaryonline.com/views/front_matter.php.

Jung, Carl G. *Collected Works of C.G. Jung, Vol.9 Part 1, Archetypes and the Collective Unconscious*. 2nd ed. Translated by R.F.C. Hull. Bollingen Series XX. Princeton: Princeton University Press, 1981.

Jung, Carl G. *Collected Works of C.G. Jung, Vol.9 Part 2, Aion: Researches into the Phenomenology of the Self*. 2nd ed. Translated by R.F.C. Hull. Bollingen Series XX. Princeton: Princeton University Press, 1979.

Jung, Carl G. *Collected Works of C. G. Jung, Vol. 14, Mysterium Coniunctionis*. Translated by R. F.C. Hull. Bollingen Series XX. Princeton: Princeton University Press, 1963.

Jung, Carl G. *Memories, Dreams, Reflections*. Edited by Aniela Jaffé. Translated by Richard and Clara Winston. New York: Vintage Books, 1963.

Jung, Carl G. *The Undiscovered Self: The Dilemma of the Individual in Modern Society* (1957). Translated by R.F.C. Hull. New York: New American Library, 2006.

Kaku, Michio. *The Future of the Mind: The Scientific Quest to Understand, Enhance, and Empower the Mind*. New York: Doubleday, 2014.

Kaku, Michio. *The Leonard Lopate Show*. WNYC, February 25, 2014.
https://www.wnyc.org/story/michio-kaku-explores-human-brain/.

Keller, Helen. *The World I Live In*. London: Hodder & Stoughton, 1904.
https://www.gutenberg.org/files/27683/27683-h/27683-h.htm.

Kennedy, Susan Ariel Rainbow (aka SARK). *Prosperity Pie: How to Relax About Money and Everything Else*. New York: Simon and Schuster, 2002.

Kenny, Anthony J. P. "Philosophy of Mind of Aristotle."
https://www.britannica.com/biography/Aristotle/Philosophy-of-mind.

Keysers, Christian, and Valeria Gazzola. "Hebbian Learning and Predictive Mirror Neurons for Actions, Sensations and Emotions." *Philosophical Transactions* 28, 2014. https://doi.org/10.1098/rstb.2013.0175.

Kinsman, Francis. *Millennium: Towards Tomorrow's Society*. London: W.H. Allen, 1989.

Kinzer, Stephen. *Poisoner in Chief: Sidney Gottlieb and the CIA Search for Mind Control*. New York: Henry Holt and Co., 2019.

Krishnamurti, Jiddu. Public Talk 3 in Ojai, California, April 14, 1973.
https://jkrishnamurti.org/content/mind-full-conclusions-dead-mind-living-mind-free-mi.

Lao Tzu. *Tao Te Ching*. 1988. Translated by Stephen Mitchell. New York: HarperCollins Digital Edition, 2004.

Levitin, Daniel J. *The Organized Mind : Thinking Straight in the Age Of Information Overload*.
New York: Penguin, 2014.

Loftus, E.F. "Leading Questions and the Eyewitness Report." *Cognitive Psychology* 7, no. 4 (1975): 560–572.
https://doi.org/10.1016/0010-0285(75)90023-7.

Lovelace, Ada. Letter to Charles Babbage, 5 July 1843. British Library, Add. Mss. 37192, ff. 350–3.

Ma Jaya Sati Bhagavati. *The 11 Karmic Spaces: Choosing Freedom From the Patterns That Bind You*.
Sebastian, FL: Kashi Publishing, 2012.

Maslow, Abraham H. *The Psychology of Science: A Reconnaissance*.
Anna Maria, FL: Maurice Bassett Publishing, 1966.

Maté, Gabor. *The Myth of Normal*. New York: Penguin Random House 2022.

McKenna, Terence. Interview with Lorenzo Hagerty, Psychedelic Salon podcast "Under the Teaching Tree"
Part 3, 2010. https://psychedelicsalon.com/podcast-217-mckenna-under-the-teaching-tree1-part-3/.

McLaren, Karla. *Emotional Genius : Discovering the Deepest Language of the Soul*.
Santa Rosa, CA: Laughing Tree Press, 2001.

Megginson, Leon C. "Lessons from Europe for American Business." Southwestern Social Science
Quarterly 44, no. 1 (1963): 3–13. https://www.jstor.org/stable/42866937.

Missinne, Stefaan. *The Da Vinci Globe*. Newcastle upon Tyne, United Kingdom:
Cambridge Scholars Publishing, 2018.

Monroe, Douglas. *The 21 Lessons of Merlyn: A Study in Druid Magic & Lore*.
St Paul, MN: Llewellyn Publications, 2004.

Moszkowski, Alexander. *Conversations with Einstein*. 1920. Translated by Henry L. Brose.
New York: Horizon Press, 1970.

Murphy, Joseph. *The Power of Your Subconscious Mind: Unlock the Secrets Within*.
London: Penguin Books, 2011.

Ong, L.M.L., J.C.J.M. de Haes, A.M. Hoos, and F.B. Lammes. "Doctor-Patient Communication:
A Review of the Literature." *Social Science & Medicine* 40, no. 7 (1995): 903–918.
https://doi.org/10.1016/0277-9536(94)00155-M.

Open University. "Psychological Research, Obedience and Ethics." https://www.open.edu/openlearn/society-
politics-law/sociology/psychological-research-obedience-and-ethics/.

Orlowski, Jeff, dir. *The Social Dilemma*. Netflix, 2020.

Pascual-Leone, A., D. Nguyet, L. G. Cohen, J. P. Brasil-Neto, A. Cammarota, and M. Hallett. "Modulation of Muscle Responses Evoked by Transcranial Magnetic Stimulation During the Acquisition of New Fine Motor Skills." *Journal of Neurophysiology* 74, no. 3 (1995): 1037–1045. https://doi.org/10.1152/jn.1995.74.3.1037.

Parkhill, Stephen C. *Answer Cancer.* Deerfield Beach, FL: Health Communications, 1995.

Peale, Norman Vincent. *The Power of Positive Thinking.* Greenwich, CT: Fawcett Publications, 1965.

Penrose, Roger. "Why Consciousness Does Not Compute." Interview by Steve Paulson. Nautilus, April 27, 2017. https://nautil.us/roger-penrose-on-why-consciousness-does-not-compute-236591/.

Person, Hannibal, and Laurie Keefer. "Psychological Comorbidity in Gastrointestinal Diseases: Update on the Brain-Gut-Microbiome Axis." *Progress in Neuro-Psychopharmacology and Biological Psychiatry* 107, no. 110209, 2021. https://doi.org/10.1016/j.pnpbp.2020.110209.

Philpotts, Eden. *A Shadow Passes.* London: C. Palmer & Hayward, 1918.

Polan, H. Jonathan, and Mary J. Ward. "Role of the Mother's Touch in Failure to Thrive: A Preliminary Investigation," *Journal of the American Academy of Child & Adolescent Psychiatry* 33, no. 8 (1994): 1098–1105. https://doi.org/10.1097/00004583-199410000-00005.

Proust, Marcel. *In Search of Lost Time. The Complete Masterpiece.* Translated by C. K. Scott Moncrieff and Terence Kilmartin. New York: Modern Library eBook Edition, 1981.

Roland, Elisa. "13 World-Changing Ideas That Came from Dreams (Literally)." *Reader's Digest*, 2021. https://www.readersdigest.com.au/true-stories-lifestyle/history/13-world-changing-ideas-came-dreams-literally.

Ruiz, Don Miguel. *The Four Agreements: A Practical Guide to Personal Freedom.* San Rafael, CA: Amber-Allen Publishing, 1997.

Schredl, Michael , and Daniel Erlacher. "Self-Reported Effects of Dreams on Waking-Life Creativity: An Empirical Study." *The Journal of Psychology* 141, no. 1 (2007): 35-46. https://doi.org/10.3200/JRLP.141.1.35-46.

Sharp, Peter. *Nurturing Emotional Literacy.* London: David Fulton Publishers, 2001.

Siegel, Dan. "The Self is Not Defined by the Boundaries of Our Skin," *Psychology Today*, February 28, 2014. https://www.psychologytoday.com/intl/blog/inspire-rewire/201402/the-self-is-not-defined-the-boundaries-our-skin.

Soroka, Stuart, Patrick Fournier, and Lilach Nir. "Cross-National Evidence of a Negativity Bias in Psychophysiological Reactions to News." *Proceedings of the National Academy of Sciences* (*PNAS*) 116, no. 38 (September 3, 2019): 18888–18892. https://doi.org/10.1073/pnas.1908369116.

Spence, Charles. "The Tongue Map and the Spatial Modulation of Taste Perception,"
   Current Research in Food Science 5 (2022): 598–610. https://doi.org/10.1016/j.crfs.2022.02.004.

Stamets, Paul. *Mycelium Running: How Mushrooms Can Help Save the World.*
   Berkeley, CA: Ten Speed Press, 2005.

The UNESCO Courier. "Leonardo da Vinci's Aphorisms and Fables." April 1952.
   https://en.unesco.org/courier/abril-1952/leonardo-da-vinci-s-aphorisms-and-fables.

Thoreau, Henry David. Journal entry, 7 July 1851. Reprinted in *Thoreau and the Art of Life:*
   Precepts and Principles. Bristol, VT: Heron Dance Press, 2006.

Thoreau, Henry David. *Walden* and "Civil Disobedience." 2nd ed. Edited by William Rossi.
   New York: W. W. Norton & Company, 1992.

Three Initiates. *The Kybalion: A Study of The Hermetic Philosophy of Ancient Egypt and Greece.*
   Chicago: The Yogi Publication Society, 1908.

Vance, Erik. *Suggestible You: The Curious Science of Your Brain's Ability to Deceive, Transform, and Heal.*
   Narrated by Richard Powers. Ashland, OR: Blackstone Audio, 2016.

Vărășteanu, Carmen-Mihaela, and Alina Iftime. "The Role of the Self-Esteem, Emotional Intelligence,
   Performance Triad in Obtaining School Satisfaction." *Procedia–Social and Behavioral Sciences* 93, 2013.
   https://doi.org./10.1016/j.sbspro.2013.10.125.

Viereck, George. S. "What Life Means to Einstein." *Saturday Evening Post*, 26 October 1929.
   Reprinted in George S. Viereck, *Glimpses of the Great.* New York: Macauley, 1930.

Walker, Matthew P., and Els van der Helm. "Overnight Therapy? The Role of Sleep in Emotional
   Brain Processing." *Psychological Bulletin* 135, no. 5 (2009): 731–748.
   https://psycnet.apa.org/doi/10.1037/a0016570.

Wilber, Ken. *The Spectrum of Consciousness.* London: Theosophical Publishing House, 1977.

Williams, Lawrence E., and John A. Bargh. "Experiencing Physical Warmth Promotes Interpersonal
   Warmth." *Science* 322, no. 5901 (2008): 606–607. https://doi.org/10.1126/science.1162548.

Wittgenstein, Ludwig. *Zettel.* Oakland, CA: University of California Press, 1967.

Wolfe, Linnie Marsh, ed. *John of the Mountains: The Unpublished Journals of John Muir.* 2nd ed.,
   Madison, WI: University of Wisconsin Press, 1979.

Yogananda, Paramahansa. *Autobiography of a Yogi.* Los Angeles: Self-Realization Fellowship, 2014.

Zeidman, Peter, and Eleanor A. Maguire. "Anterior Hippocampus: The Anatomy of Perception,
   Imagination and Episodic Memory." *Nature Reviews Neuroscience* 17 (2016): 173–182.
   https://doi.org/10.1038/nrn.2015.24.

Notes

Introduction

1   Gabor Maté, *The Myth of Normal* (New York: Penguin Random House 2022), chapter 30.

2   Roger Penrose, "Why Consciousness Does Not Compute," interview by Steve Paulson, Nautilus, April 27, 2017. https://nautil.us/roger-penrose-on-why-consciousness-does-not-compute-236591/.

What is Mind?

3   Paul Stamets, *Mycelium Running: How Mushrooms Can Help Save the World* (Berkeley, CA: Ten Speed Press, 2005), 7.

4   Albert Einstein, *Essays in Science* (1934), translated by Alan Harris (Mineola, NY: Dover Publications, 2009), 11.

5   Dan Siegel, "The Self is Not Defined by the Boundaries of Our Skin," *Psychology Today*, February 28, 2014. https://www.psychologytoday.com/intl/blog/inspire-rewire/201402/the-self-is-not-defined-the-boundaries-our-skin.

6   Three Initiates, *The Kybalion: A Study of The Hermetic Philosophy of Ancient Egypt and Greece* (Chicago: The Yogi Publication Society, 1908), 26.

7   Lao Tzu, *Tao Te Ching*, translated by Stephen Mitchell (New York: HarperCollins Digital Edition, 2004).

8   *The Dhammapada*, translated from Pāli by F. Max Müller (London: Curzon Press, 1870; Abingdon-on-Thames, Oxfordshire: Routledge, 2013), 25–26. Citation refers to the Routledge edition.

9   Anthony J. P. Kenny, "Philosophy of Mind of Aristotle." https://www.britannica.com/biography/Aristotle/Philosophy-of-mind.

10   Rene Descartes, *Discourse on Method* (1637). https://brians.wsu.edu/2016/11/04/rene-descartes-discourse-on-method-1637/.

11   Ada Lovelace to Charles Babbage, letter July 5, 1843, British Library, Add. Mss. 37192, ff. 350–3, quoted in Lawrence Goldman, *Victorians and Numbers: Statistics and Society in Nineteenth Century Britain* (New York: Oxford University Press, 2009), 124.

12   As quoted in Norman Vincent Peale, *The Power of Positive Thinking* (Greenwich, CT: Fawcett Publications, 1965), 167.

13   Paraphrased from *The Interpretation of Dreams* (*Die Traumdeutung*), first published in 1899.

14   Douglas Monroe, *The 21 Lessons of Merlyn: A Study in Druid Magic & Lore* (St Paul, MN: Llewellyn Publications, 2004), 33.

15   Jane Goodall, *Harvest for Hope* (New York: Hachette Book Group, 2005), chapter 19.

Hardware

16   Michio Kaku, *The Future of the Mind : The Scientific Quest to Understand, Enhance,
and Empower the Mind* (Doubleday, 2014), chapter 11.

17   Michio Kaku, interview by Leonard Lopate, *The Leonard Lopate Show*, WNYC, February 25, 2014.
https://www.wnyc.org/story/michio-kaku-explores-human-brain/.

Software: The Conscious Mind

18   Carl Jung, *Collected Works of C. G. Jung*, translated by R. F.C. Hull, vol. 14,
Mysterium Coniunctionis, Bollingen Series XX (Princeton: Princeton University Press, 1963), 359.

19   Henry David Thoreau, July 7, 1851 journal entry, reprinted in *Thoreau and the Art of Life:
Precepts and Principles* (Bristol, VT: Heron Dance Press, 2006), 27.

20   Public talk 3 in Ojai, California, April 14, 1973.
https://jkrishnamurti.org/content/mind-full-conclusions-dead-mind-living-mind-free-mi.

21   William James, "Is Life Worth Living?" *International Journal of Ethics* 6, no. 1, 1895.
https://www.jstor.org/stable/2375619.

22   Nancy Colier, "Negative Thinking: A Dangerous Addiction," *Psychology Today*, April 15, 2019.
https://www.psychologytoday.com/za/blog/inviting-monkey-tea/201904/negative-thinking-
dangerous-addiction.

23   Stuart Soroka, Patrick Fournier, and Lilach Nir, "Cross-National Evidence of a Negativity Bias in
Psychophysiological Reactions to News," *Proceedings of the National Academy of Sciences* (*PNAS*)
116, no. 38 (September 3, 2019): 18888-18892. https://doi.org/10.1073/pnas.1908369116.

24   William James, *Pragmatism: A New Name for Some Old Ways of Thinking*
(London: Longmans, Green, and Company, 1909).

25   Paraphrased from Napoleon Hill, *How to Own Your Own Mind*
(New York: TarcherPerigee, 2017), Chapter 2 (Organized Thought).

26   K. Sri Dhammananda, *How to Live Without Fear and Worry*
(Malaysia, Buddhist Missionary Society,1989), 192.

27   Napoleon Hill, *How to Own Your Own Mind* (New York: TarcherPerigee, 2017),
Chapter 3 (Controlled Attention).

28   Daniel Goleman, "Has Attention Shrunk?" ch. 2 in *Focus: The Hidden Driver of Excellence*
(New York: HarperCollins, 2013).

29   Daniel J. Levitin, "Too Much Information, Too Many Decisions," ch. 1 in *The Organized Mind: Thinking Straight in the Age Of Information Overload* (New York: Penguin, 2014).

30   Louis Mayeul Chaudon, *Historical and Critical Memoirs of the Life and Writings of M. De Voltaire* (London: G. G. J and J. Robinson, 1786), 291.

31   Waqās Ahmed, "The Mind of Leonardo da Vinci," *Philosophy Now* 134 (2019). https://philosophynow.org/issues/134/The_Mind_of_Leonardo_da_Vinci.

32   As quoted in Carmen-Mihaela Vărășteanu and Alina Iftime, "The Role of the Self-Esteem, Emotional Intelligence, Performance Triad in Obtaining School Satisfaction," *Procedia—Social and Behavioral Sciences* 93 (2013). https://doi.org./10.1016/j.sbspro.2013.10.125.

33   Christian Keysers and Valeria Gazzola, "Hebbian Learning and Predictive Mirror Neurons for Actions, Sensations and Emotions." *Philosophical Transactions* 28 (2014). https://doi.org/10.1098/rstb.2013.0175.

34   Michael Inzlicht, Elliot Berkman, and Nathaniel Elkins-Brown, "The Neuroscience of 'Ego Depletion' or: How the Brain Can Help Us Understand Why Self-Control Seems Limited," in *Social Neuroscience Biological Approaches to Social Psychology*, edited by Eddie Harmon-Jones and Michael Inzlicht (New York: Taylor & Francis, 2016), 102.

35   Benjamin C. Ampel, Mark Muraven, and Ewan C. McNay, "Mental Work Requires Physical Energy: Self-Control Is Neither Exception nor Exceptional," *Frontiers in Psychology* 9, article 1005 (2018). https://doi.org/10.3389/fpsyg.2018.01005.

Software: The Subconscious Mind

36   Max Beckett, "History of the Internet: A Timeline Throughout the Years," July 6, 2023. https://www.uswitch.com/broadband/guides/broadband-history/.

37   Paraphrased from: William James, *The Varieties of Religious Experience* (1902), reprinted by Delphi Classics, 2018.

38   Waqās Ahmed, "The Mind of Leonardo da Vinci," *Philosophy Now* 134 (2019). https://philosophynow.org/issues/134/The_Mind_of_Leonardo_da_Vinci.

39   Eden Philpotts, *A Shadow Passes* (London: C. Palmer & Hayward, 1918).

40   Alexandra Horowitz, *Being a Dog: Following the Dog Into a World of Smell* (New York: Scribner, 2016).

41   Richard E. Cytowic, and David M. Eagleman, *Wednesday is Indigo Blue: Discovering the Brain of Synesthesia* (Cambridge: Massachusetts Institute of Technology, 2009).

42   Helen Keller, *The World I Live In* (London: Hodder & Stoughton, 1904). https://www.gutenberg.org/files/27683/27683-h/27683-h.htm.

43   Maaike J. de Bruijn and Michael Bender, "Olfactory Cues Are More Effective Than Visual Cues in Experimentally Triggering Autobiographical Memories," *Memory* 26, no. 4 (2018). https://doi.org/10.1080/09658211.2017.1381744.

44   Ophélie Glachet and Mohamad El Haj, "Odor Is More Effective Than a Visual Cue or a Verbal Cue for The Recovery of Autobiographical Memories in AD," *Journal of Clinical and Experimental Neuropsychology* 43, no. 2 (2021): 129–143. https://doi.org/10.1080/13803395.2021.1882392.

45   Charles Spence, "The Tongue Map and the Spatial Modulation of Taste Perception," *Current Research in Food Science* 5 (2022): 598–610. https://doi.org/10.1016/j.crfs.2022.02.004.

46   Rick Chillot, "The Power of Touch," *Psychology Today*, March 11, 2013. https://www.psychologytoday.com/articles/the-power-of-touch.

47   H. Jonathan Polan, and Mary J. Ward, "Role of the Mother's Touch in Failure to Thrive: A Preliminary Investigation," *Journal of the American Academy of Child & Adolescent Psychiatry* 33, no. 8 (1994): 1098–1105. https://doi.org/10.1097/00004583-199410000-00005.

48   Jeffrey D. Fisher, Marvin Rytting and Richard Heslin, "Hands Touching Hands: Affective and Evaluative Effects of an Interpersonal Touch," *Sociometry* 39, no. 4 (1976): 416–421. https://doi.org/10.2307/3033506.

49   Lawrence E. Williams and John A. Bargh, "Experiencing Physical Warmth Promotes Interpersonal Warmth," Science 322, no. 5901 (2008): 606–607. https://doi.org/10.1126/science.1162548.

50   Tiffany Field, *Touch*, 2nd ed. (Cambridge: MIT Press, 2014), 6.

51   L.M.L. Ong, et al., "Doctor-Patient Communication: A Review of the Literature," *Social Science & Medicine* 40, no. 7 (1995): 903–918. https://doi.org/10.1016/0277-9536(94)00155-M.

52   Ryuji Hirayama et al., "High-Speed Acoustic Holography with Arbitrary Scattering Objects," *Science Advances* 8, no. 24 (2022). https://doi.org/10.1126/sciadv.abn7614.

53   Hannibal Person and Laurie Keefer, "Psychological Comorbidity in Gastrointestinal Diseases: Update on the Brain-Gut-Microbiome Axis," *Progress in Neuro-Psychopharmacology and Biological Psychiatry* 107, no. 110209 (2021). https://doi.org/10.1016/j.pnpbp.2020.110209.

54   Joe Dispenza, "The Placebo Effect in the Brain," ch. 3 in *You Are the Placebo: Making Your Mind Matter* (Carlsbad, CA: Hay House, 2014).

55   E.F. Loftus, "Leading Questions and the Eyewitness Report," *Cognitive Psychology* 7. no. 4: 560–572 (1975). https://doi.org/10.1016/0010-0285(75)90023-7.

56   Terence McKenna, interview with Lorenzo Hagerty, Psychedelic Salon podcast "Under the Teaching Tree" Part 3, 2010. https://psychedelicsalon.com/podcast-217-mckenna-under-the-teaching-tree1-part-3/.

57   See Carmine Gallo, "The Maya Angelou Quote That Will Radically Improve Your Business," *Forbes*, May 31, 2014. https://www.forbes.com/sites/carminegallo/2014/05/31/the-maya-angelou-quote-that-will-radically-improve-your-business/.

58   Benedict de Spinoza, Part V: Of the Power of the Understanding, or of Human Freedom, Proposition III, in *Ethics*. https://www.gutenberg.org/files/3800/3800-h/3800-h.htm.

59   Benedict de Spinoza, *The Chief Works of Benedict de Spinoza*, translated from Latin, with an introduction by R.H.M. Elwes (1901), 187. https://www.gutenberg.org/files/3800/3800-h/3800-h.htm

60   Sigmund Freud, *The Psychopathology of Everyday Life* (1901), translated by A. A. Brill (London: Macmillan, 1915), 333.

61   Alexander Moszkowski, *Conversations with Einstein* (1920), translated by Henry L. Brose (New York: Horizon Press, 1970).

62   George. S. Viereck, "What Life Means to Einstein," *Saturday Evening Post*, October 26, 1929. Reprinted in George S. Viereck, *Glimpses of the Great* (New York: Macauley, 1930).

63   Linnie Marsh Wolfe ed., *John of the Mountains: The Unpublished Journals of John Muir*, 2nd ed. (Madison, WI: University of Wisconsin Press, 1879), 226.

64   *The UNESCO Courier*, "Leonardo da Vinci's Aphorisms and Fables," April 1952. https://en.unesco.org/courier/abril-1952/leonardo-da-vinci-s-aphorisms-and-fables.

65   Peter Zeidman, and Eleanor A. Maguire, "Anterior Hippocampus: The Anatomy of Perception, Imagination and Episodic Memory," *Nature Reviews Neuroscience* 17 (2016): 176. https://doi.org/10.1038/nrn.2015.24.

66   A. Pascual-Leone et al., "Modulation of Muscle Responses Evoked by Transcranial Magnetic Stimulation During the Acquisition of New Fine Motor Skills," *Journal of Neurophysiology* 74, no. 3 (1995): 1037-1045. https://doi.org/10.1152/jn.1995.74.3.1037.

67   Michael Schredl, and Daniel Erlacher "Self-Reported Effects of Dreams on Waking-Life Creativity: An Empirical Study," *The Journal of Psychology* 141, no. 1 (2007): 43. https://doi.org/10.3200/JRLP.141.1.35-46.

68   Matthew P. Walker, and Els van der Helm. "Overnight Therapy? The Role of Sleep in Emotional Brain Processing," *Psychological Bulletin* 135, no. 5 (2009): 741. https://psycnet.apa.org/doi/10.1037/a0016570.

69   Elisa Roland, "13 World-Changing Ideas That Came from Dreams (Literally)," *Reader's Digest* (2021). https://www.readersdigest.com.au/true-stories-lifestyle/history/13-world-changing-ideas-came-dreams-literally.

70   Henry David Thoreau, *Walden* and "Civil Disobedience," 2nd ed., edited by William Rossi
(New York: W. W. Norton & Company, 1992), 90.

71   Philip Gross, "The Same River: Thirteen Variations on Heraclitus," *New Writing* 10, no. 3 (2013): 312.
https://doi.org/10.1080/14790726.2013.804844.

72   Michael J. Gelb, *How to Think Like Leonardo Da Vinci* (New York: Random House, 2004).

How to Change Your Mind: How You Think and Feel

73   Leon C. Megginson, "Lessons from Europe for American Business," *Southwestern Social Science
Quarterly* 44, no. 1 (1963): 3-13. https://www.jstor.org/stable/42866937.

74   As quoted in Francis Kinsman, *Millennium: Towards Tomorrow's Society*
(London: W.H. Allen, 1989), 223.

75   Samuel Johnson, preface to *A Dictionary of the English Language* (1755), 2.
https://johnsonsdictionaryonline.com/views/front_matter.php.

76   Carl G. Jung, *Memories, Dreams, Reflections*, edited by Aniela Jaffé and translated by
Richard & Clara Winston (New York: Vintage Books, 1963), 326.

77   William Blake, *The Marriage of Heaven and Hell* (1790).
https://www.gutenberg.org/files/45315/45315-h/45315-h.htm.

78   Rephrased from Jung's explanation that "The psychological rule says that when an inner situation is
not made conscious, it happens outside, as fate. That is to say, when the individual remains undivided
and does not become conscious of his inner opposite, the world must perforce act out the conflict
and be torn into opposing halves." Carl G. Jung, *Collected Works*, 2nd ed., translated by R. F.C. Hull,
Vol. 9 Part 2, *Aion: Researches into the Phenomenology of the Self*, Bollingen Series XX
(Princeton: Princeton University Press, 1979), 71.

79   Lao Tzu, *Tao Te Ching*, translated by Stephen Mitchell (New York: HarperCollins Digital Edition, 2004).

80   Lyndall Briggs and Gary Green, *Soul Purpose: Self Development Stories, Quotes and Poems*
(Kingsgrove, NSW: SelfDevelopment.biz, 2003), 23.

81   Marion Zimmer Bradley, *The Mists of Avalon* (New York: Ballantine Books, 1982).

82   Abraham H. Maslow, *The Psychology of Science: A Reconnaissance*
(Anna Maria, FL: Maurice Bassell Publishing, 1966), 15.

83   Tenzin Gyatso, the Fourteenth Dalai Lama, *The Wheel of Life: Buddhist Perspectives on Cause
and Effect*, rev. ed., translation by Jeffrey Hopkins of lectures given in London, 1984
(Somerville, MA: Wisdom Publications, 2015), 34.

84   Susan Ariel Rainbow Kennedy (aka SARK), *Prosperity Pie: How to Relax About Money and Everything Else* (New York: Simon and Schuster, 2002), 43.

85   Ludwig Wittgenstein, *Zettel* (Oakland, CA: University of California Press, 1967), § 55.

86   Don Miguel Ruiz, *The Four Agreements: A Practical Guide to Personal Freedom* (San Rafael, CA: Amber-Allen Publishing, 1997).

87   Napoleon Hill, *How to Own Your Own Mind* (New York: TarcherPerigee, 2017).

88   James Clear, "The Mistake Smart People Make: Being In Motion vs. Taking Action," 2020. https://jamesclear.com/taking-action.

89   Fyodor Dostoevsky, *The Possessed* (1916), translated by Constance Garnett (Project Gutenberg, 2005). https://www.gutenberg.org/files/8117/8117-h/8117-h.htm.

90   Jack Canfield, Mark Victor Hansen, and Les Hewitt, "Your Habits Will Determine Your Future," ch. 1 in *The Power of Focus* (New York: Random House, 2013).

91   James Clear, "3-2-1: Consistency, Anger, and Shaping the World," November 24, 2022. https://jamesclear.com/3-2-1/november-24-2022.

92   As quoted in David C. Batman. 2012. "Hippocrates: Walking is Man's Best Medicine!" *Occupational Medicine* 62, no. 5 (2012): 320–322. https://doi.org/10.1093/occmed/kqs084.

93   Andrew Huberman, and Joe Dispenza, "Feeling Stuck?" Reprogram Yourself, YouTube video, May 1, 2023. https://www.youtube.com/watch?v=CjQo7DebOgs.

How to Fortify Your Mind

94   Ralph Waldo Emerson, "Self-Reliance," in *Essays: First Series* (1841). https://archive.vcu.edu/english/engweb/transcendentalism/authors/emerson/essays/.

95   As quoted in György Buzsáki, *The Brain from Inside Out* (New York: Oxford University Press, 2018), 1.

96   Robert B. Cialdini, *Influence: The Psychology of Persuasion*, rev. ed. (New York: Harper Business, 2006).

97   Winston Churchill, *Onwards to Victory: War Speeches*, compiled by Charles Eade (Cassell and Co., 1943). Speech delivered at Harvard University, September 6, 1943, https://www.harvardmagazine.com/2018/09/churchill-harvard-september-6-1943.

98   The Open University provides a clear explanation of the experiments in their course on Psychological Research, Obedience and Ethics at https://www.open.edu/openlearn/society-politics-law/sociology/psychological-research-obedience-and-ethics/.

99   Jeff Orlowski, dir., *The Social Dilemma,* Netflix, 2020.

100   Noam Chomsky, "The 5 Filters of the Mass Media Machine,"
        YouTube video, March 2, 2017. https://www.youtube.com/watch?v=34LGPIXvU5M.

101   Stephen Kinzer, *Poisoner in Chief: Sidney Gottlieb and the CIA Search for Mind Control*
        (New York: Henry Holt and Co., 2019), chapter 5.

102   Stephen Kinzer, chapter 11.

103   Elmer Green, "Beyond Psychophysics," *Subtle Energies & Energy Medicine* 10, no. 1 (1999): 368.
        https://journals.sfu.ca/seemj/index.php/seemj/article/view/290.

**Visit us by scanning the QR code or
www.mindmoodvibe.com/mmvpress/mindmanual/source**
for up to date and extended materials along with all the
original source links in one place.

About the Author

Meet April Norris–A passionate advocate for unleashing the power of the subconscious mind. With over 25 years of experience as a Board Certified Hypnotherapist and Master Hypnosis Trainer, April has guided thousands on their journey to discover the root cause of their issues and achieve mental and emotional freedom in just a few sessions. From healing anxiety, trauma, and illness through medical hypnosis to teaching university students and healthcare professionals about the profound healing potential of the mind, her expertise spans the most transformative corners of mind-body connection.

April considers the science of mind training to be an artform, combining cutting-edge techniques with a deep understanding of how our thoughts shape our reality. She's a sought-after coach for leaders and visionaries, helping them unlock their potential and create lasting impact. April also leads immersive retreats, guiding participants through transformative experiences that elevate their mindset and spark profound inner growth.

In her spare time, when she's not helping others unlock their mind's potential, you'll find her bouncing ideas (and herself) on her big trampoline—because sometimes, life's best breakthroughs happen mid-jump.

You can learn more about her work at:
www.mindmoodvibe.com

9 798993 855134